Praise for *Poems New and Collected*

"Szymborska struggles for the utmost [
gages in complicated linguistic game
of her native tongue. . . . A superb English translation

—*Los Angeles Times Book Review*

"Szymborska is an intellectually supple but accessible poet, and her translators are sensitive to the lyrical limberness of [her] verse."

—*The Boston Sunday Globe*

"A major poet whose dark, complex and profoundly intelligent work might otherwise have remained lost to us. Szymborska is a poet who comes across unusually well in translation, for her poetry is made as much of images and ideas, their manipulation and unlikely juxtaposition, as of the untranslatable nuances of words."

— *The Washington Post*

"It may seem superfluous to praise a Nobel laureate in literature, but Szymborska is a writer richly deserving of her recent renown. She has no counterpart in English verse. An essential purchase for all interested in literature."

—*Library Journal*

"With the release of Szymborska's *Poems: New and Collected*, [we have] the most complete English language edition available of the work by the Nobel Prize–winning Polish poet. American poet Robert Hass has said, 'she is unquestionably one of the greatest living European poets. She's accessible and deeply human and a joy—though it is a dark kind of joy.'"

—*Houston Chronicle*

"Szymborska has become, with the suddenness of a shot of lightening, a necessary presence in modern literature, without whom our world has until now been the poorer."

—*The Boston Phoenix*

Poems
New and Collected
1957–1997

WISŁAWA SZYMBORSKA

Poems
New and Collected
1957–1997

Translated from the Polish
by Stanisław Barańczak and Clare Cavanagh

A HARVEST BOOK
HARCOURT, INC.
San Diego   New York   London

All poems from *View with a Grain of Sand, Selected Poems*
appear in this volume.

Library of Congress Cataloging-in-Publication Data
Szymborska, Wisława.
[Poems, English]
Poems new and collected 1957–1977/Wisława Szymborska
translated from the Polish by Stanisław Barańczak and Clare Cavanagh.—1st ed.
p. cm.
ISBN 0-15-100353-X
ISBN 0-15-601146-8 (pbk.)
1. Szymborska, Wisława—Translations into English.
I. Barańczak, Stanisław, 1946–. II. Cavanagh, Clare. III. Title.
PG7178.Z9A222 1998
891.8'517—dc21 97-32277

Text set in Bembo
Designed by Lori McThomas Buley
Printed in the United States of America
First Harvest edition 2000
E F D

CONTENTS

NO END OF FUN 1967

from COULD HAVE 1972

from A LARGE NUMBER 1976

THE PEOPLE ON THE BRIDGE 1986

THE END AND THE BEGINNING 1993

NEW POEMS 1993–97

The Poet and the World

Nobel Lecture
1996

They say that the first sentence in any speech is always the hardest. Well, that one's behind me. But I have a feeling that the sentences to come—the third, the sixth, the tenth, and so on, up to the final line—will be just as hard, since I'm supposed to talk about poetry. I've said very little on the subject—next to nothing, in fact. And whenever I have said anything, I've always had the sneaking suspicion that I'm not very good at it. This is why my lecture will be rather short. Imperfection is easier to tolerate in small doses.

Contemporary poets are skeptical and suspicious even, or perhaps especially, about themselves. They publicly confess to being poets only reluctantly, as if they were a little ashamed of it. But in our clamorous times it's much easier to acknowledge your faults, at least if they're attractively packaged, than to recognize your own merits, since these are hidden deeper and you never quite believe in them yourself. When they fill out questionnaires or chat with strangers—that is, when they can't avoid revealing their profession—poets prefer to use the general term "writer" or replace "poet" with the name of whatever job they do in addition to writing. Bureaucrats and bus passengers respond with a touch of incredulity and alarm when they discover that they're dealing with a poet. I suppose philosophers meet with a similar reaction. Still, they are in a better position, since as often as not they can embellish their calling with some kind of scholarly title. Professor of philosophy: now that sounds much more respectable.

But there are no professors of poetry. That would mean, after all, that poetry is an occupation requiring specialized study, regular examinations, theoretical articles with bibliographies and footnotes attached, and, finally, ceremoniously conferred diplomas. And this would mean, in turn, that it's not enough to cover pages with even the most exquisite poems in order to become a poet. The crucial element is some slip of paper bearing an official stamp. Let us recall that the pride of Russian poetry, the future Nobel Laureate Joseph Brodsky, was once sentenced to internal exile precisely on such grounds. They called him "a parasite," because he lacked official certification granting him the right to be a poet.

Several years ago, I had the honor and the pleasure of meeting Brodsky. And I noticed that, of all the poets I've known, he was the only one who enjoyed calling himself a poet. He pronounced the word without inhibitions. Just the opposite: he spoke it with defiant freedom. This must have been, it seems to me, because he recalled the brutal humiliations that he experienced in his youth.

In more fortunate countries, where human dignity isn't assaulted so readily, poets yearn, of course, to be published, read, and understood, but they do little, if anything, to set themselves above the common herd and the daily grind. And yet it wasn't so long ago, it was in this century's first decades, that poets strove to shock us with their extravagant dress and eccentric behavior. But all this was merely for the sake of public display. The moment always came when poets had to close the doors behind them, strip off their mantles, fripperies, and other poetic paraphernalia, and confront—silently, patiently awaiting their own selves—the still-white sheet of paper. For finally this is what really counts.

It's not accidental that film biographies of great scientists and artists are produced in droves. The more ambitious directors seek to reproduce convincingly the creative process that led to important scientific discoveries or to the emergence of a masterpiece. And one can depict certain kinds of scientific labor with some success. Laboratories, sundry instruments, elaborate machinery brought to life:

such scenes may hold the audience's interest for a while. And those moments of uncertainty—will the experiment, conducted for the thousandth time with some tiny modification, finally yield the desired result?—can be quite dramatic. Films about painters can be spectacular, as they go about recreating every stage of a famous painting's evolution, from the first penciled line to the final brushstroke. And music swells in films about composers: the first bars of the melody that rings in the musician's ears finally emerge as a mature work in symphonic form. Of course this is all quite naïve and doesn't explain the strange mental state popularly known as inspiration, but at least there's something to look at and listen to.

But poets are the worst. Their work is hopelessly unphotogenic. Someone sits at a table or lies on a sofa while staring motionless at a wall or ceiling. Once in a while this person writes down seven lines, only to cross out one of them fifteen minutes later, and then another hour passes, during which nothing happens. . . . Who could stand to watch this kind of thing?

I've mentioned inspiration. Contemporary poets answer evasively when asked what it is, and if it actually exists. It's not that they've never known the blessing of this inner impulse. It's just not easy to explain to someone else what you don't understand yourself.

When I'm asked about this on occasion, I hedge, too. But my answer is this: Inspiration is not the exclusive privilege of poets or artists. There is, there has been, there will always be a certain group of people whom inspiration visits. It's made up of all those who've consciously chosen their calling and do their job with love and imagination. It may include doctors, teachers, gardeners—I could list a hundred more professions. Their work becomes one continuous adventure as long as they manage to keep discovering new challenges in it. Difficulties and setbacks never quell their curiosity. A swarm of new questions emerges from every problem that they solve. Whatever inspiration is, it's born from a continuous "I don't know."

There aren't many such people. Most of the earth's inhabitants work to get by. They work because they have to. They didn't pick this or that kind of job out of passion; the circumstances of their lives did the choosing for them. Loveless work, boring work, work valued only because others haven't got even that much—this is one of the harshest human miseries. And there's no sign that coming centuries will produce any changes for the better as far as this goes.

And so, though I deny poets their monopoly on inspiration, I still place them in a select group of Fortune's darlings.

At this point, though, certain doubts may arise in my audience. All sorts of torturers, dictators, fanatics, and demagogues struggling for power with a few loudly shouted slogans also enjoy their jobs, and they, too, perform their duties with inventive fervor. Well, yes; but they "know," and whatever they know is enough for them once and for all. They don't want to find out about anything else, since that might diminish the force of their arguments. But any knowledge that doesn't lead to new questions quickly dies out: it fails to maintain the temperature required for sustaining life. In the most extreme cases, cases well known from ancient and modern history, it even poses a lethal threat to society.

This is why I value that little phrase "I don't know" so highly. It's small, but it flies on mighty wings. It expands our lives to include spaces within us as well as the outer expanses in which our tiny Earth hangs suspended. If Isaac Newton had never said to himself, "I don't know," the apples in his little orchard might have dropped to the ground like hailstones, and at best he would have stooped to pick them up and gobble them with gusto. Had my compatriot Marie Skłodowska-Curie never said to herself, "I don't know," she probably would have wound up teaching chemistry at some private high school for young ladies from good families and ended her days performing this otherwise perfectly respectable job. But she kept on saying, "I don't know," and these words led her, not just once but twice, to Stockholm, where restless, questing spirits are occasionally rewarded with the Nobel Prize.

Poets, if they're genuine, must also keep repeating, "I don't know." Each poem marks an effort to answer this statement, but as soon as the final period hits the page, the poet begins to hesitate, starts to realize that this particular answer was pure makeshift, absolutely inadequate. So poets keep on trying, and sooner or later the consecutive results of their self-dissatisfaction are clipped together with a giant paperclip by literary historians and called their "oeuvres."

I sometimes dream of situations that can't possibly come true. I audaciously imagine, for example, that I get a chance to chat with Ecclesiastes, the author of that moving lament on the vanity of all human endeavors. I bow very deeply before him, because he is one of the greatest poets, for me at least. Then I grab his hand. "There's nothing new under the sun": that's what you wrote, Ecclesiastes. But you yourself were born new under the sun. And the poem you created is also new under the sun, since no one wrote it down before you. And all your readers are also new under the sun, since those who lived before you couldn't read your poem. And that cypress under which you're sitting hasn't been growing since the dawn of time. It came into being by way of another cypress similar to yours, but not exactly the same.

And Ecclesiastes, I'd also like to ask you what new thing under the sun you're planning to work on now? A further supplement to thoughts that you've already expressed? Or maybe you're tempted to contradict some of them now? In your earlier work you mentioned joy—so what if it's fleeting? So maybe your new-under-the-sun poem will be about joy? Have you taken notes yet, do you have drafts? I doubt that you'll say, "I've written everything down, I've got nothing left to add." There's no poet in the world who can say this, least of all a great poet like yourself.

The world—whatever we might think when we're terrified by its vastness and our own impotence or when we're embittered by its indifference to individual suffering, of people, animals, and perhaps even plants (for why are we so sure that plants feel no pain?); whatever we might think of its expanses pierced by the rays of stars surrounded by planets we've just begun to discover, planets already dead, still dead, we just don't know; whatever we might think of this measureless theater to which we've got reserved tickets, but tickets whose life span is laughably short, bounded as it is by two arbitrary dates; whatever else we might think of this world—it is astonishing.

But "astonishing" is an epithet concealing a logical trap. We're astonished, after all, by things that deviate from some well-known and universally acknowledged norm, from an obviousness to which we've grown accustomed. But the point is, there is no such obvious world. Our astonishment exists per se, and it isn't based on a comparison with something else.

Granted, in daily speech, where we don't stop to consider every word, we all use phrases such as "the ordinary world," "ordinary life," "the ordinary course of events." But in the language of poetry, where every word is weighed, nothing is usual or normal. Not a single stone and not a single cloud above it. Not a single day and not a single night after it. And above all, not a single existence, not anyone's existence in this world.

It looks as though poets will always have their work cut out for them.

WISŁAWA SZYMBORSKA

December 7, 1996

Stockholm

TRANSLATORS' NOTE

This book includes, in English translation, virtually all of Wisława Szymborska's poetic work to date, beginning with her third collection, *Calling Out to Yeti*, which she herself considers her actual debut, and ending with her most recent poems published thus far only in the literary press. *Calling Out to Yeti* has been presented here in an ample selection. From the other six volumes, eight poems unfortunately had to be omitted (three from *Salt*, two from *Could Have*, and three from *A Large Number*) because of specific unsurmountable problems of a technical nature involved in the translation of each.

Compared with our earlier publication, *View with a Grain of Sand: Selected Poems by Wisława Szymborska* (Harcourt, Inc., 1995), which consisted of 100 poems, this enlarged collection presents 64 more, most of them never translated into English before.

We take this opportunity to extend our belated thanks to Charles Simic, Helen Vendler, and Drenka Willen, without whose encouragement and help *View with a Grain of Sand* and, by the same token, this book might never have come into being. Special thanks go to our enthusiastically supportive families, Anna M., Anna J., and Michael, as well as Mike and Marty.

S. B. & C. C.

from

CALLING OUT TO YETI

1957

I'M WORKING ON THE WORLD

I'm working on the world,
revised, improved edition,
featuring fun for fools,
blues for brooders,
combs for bald pates,
tricks for old dogs.

Here's one chapter: The Speech
of Animals and Plants.
Each species comes, of course,
with its own dictionary.
Even a simple "Hi there,"
when traded with a fish,
makes both the fish and you
feel quite extraordinary.

The long-suspected meanings
of rustlings, chirps, and growls!
Soliloquies of forests!
The epic hoots of owls!
Those crafty hedgehogs drafting
aphorisms after dark,
while we blindly believe
they're sleeping in the park!

Time (Chapter Two) retains
its sacred right to meddle
in each earthly affair.
Still, time's unbounded power
that makes a mountain crumble,
moves seas, rotates a star,
won't be enough to tear
lovers apart: they are
too naked, too embraced,
too much like timid sparrows.

Old age is, in my book,
the price that felons pay,
so don't whine that it's steep:
you'll stay young if you're good.
Suffering (Chapter Three)
doesn't insult the body.
Death? It comes in your sleep,
exactly as it should.

When it comes, you'll be dreaming
that you don't need to breathe;
that breathless silence is
the music of the dark
and it's part of the rhythm
to vanish like a spark.

Only a death like that. A rose
could prick you harder, I suppose;
you'd feel more terror at the sound
of petals falling to the ground.

Only a world like that. To die
just that much. And to live just so.
And all the rest is Bach's fugue, played
for the time being
on a saw.

CLASSIFIEDS

WHOEVER'S found out what location
compassion (heart's imagination)
can be contacted at these days,
is herewith urged to name the place;
and sing about it in full voice,
and dance like crazy and rejoice
beneath the frail birch that appears
to be upon the verge of tears.

I TEACH silence
in all languages
through intensive examination of:
the starry sky,
the Sinanthropus' jaws,
a grasshopper's hop,
an infant's fingernails,
plankton,
a snowflake.

I RESTORE lost love.
Act now! Special offer!
You lie on last year's grass
bathed in sunlight to the chin
while winds of summers past
caress your hair and seem
to lead you in a dance.
For further details, write: "Dream."

WANTED: someone to mourn
the elderly who die
alone in old folks' homes.
Applicants, don't send forms
or birth certificates.
All papers will be torn,

no receipts will be issued
at this or later dates.

FOR PROMISES made by my spouse,
who's tricked so many with his sweet
colors and fragrances and sounds—
dogs barking, guitars in the street—
into believing that they still
might conquer loneliness and fright,
I cannot be responsible.
Mr. Day's widow, Mrs. Night.

GREETING THE SUPERSONICS

Faster than sound today,
faster than light tomorrow,
we'll turn sound into the Tortoise
and light into the Hare.

Two venerable creatures
from the ancient parable,
a noble team, since ages past
competing fair and square.

You ran so many times
across this lowly earth;
now try another course,
across the lofty blue.

The track's all yours. We won't
get in your way: by then
we will have set off chasing
ourselves rather than you.

AN EFFORT

Alack and woe, oh song: you're mocking me;
try as I may, I'll never be your red, red rose.
A rose is a rose is a rose. And you know it.

I worked to sprout leaves. I tried to take root.
I held my breath to speed things up, and waited
for the petals to enclose me.

Merciless song, you leave me with my lone,
nonconvertible, unmetamorphic body:
I'm one-time-only to the marrow of my bones.

FOUR A.M.

The hour between night and day.
The hour between toss and turn.
The hour of thirty-year-olds.

The hour swept clean for roosters' crowing.
The hour when the earth takes back its warm embrace.
The hour of cool drafts from extinguished stars.
The hour of do-we-vanish-too-without-a-trace.

Empty hour.
Hollow. Vain.
Rock bottom of all the other hours.

No one feels fine at four a.m.
If ants feel fine at four a.m.,
we're happy for the ants. And let five a.m. come
if we've got to go on living.

STILL LIFE WITH A BALLOON

Returning memories?
No, at the time of death
I'd like to see lost objects
return instead.

Avalanches of gloves,
coats, suitcases, umbrellas—
come, and I'll say at last:
What good's all this?

Safety pins, two odd combs,
a paper rose, a knife,
some string—come, and I'll say
at last: I haven't missed you.

Please turn up, key, come out,
wherever you've been hiding,
in time for me to say:
You've gotten rusty, friend!

Downpours of affidavits,
permits and questionnaires,
rain down and I will say:
I see the sun behind you.

My watch, dropped in a river,
bob up and let me seize you—
then, face to face, I'll say:
Your so-called time is up.

And lastly, toy balloon
once kidnapped by the wind—
come home, and I will say:
There are no children here.

Fly out the open window
and into the wide world;
let someone else shout "Look!"
and I will cry.

TO MY FRIENDS

Well-versed in the expanses
that stretch from earth to stars,
we get lost in the space
from earth up to our skull.

Intergalactic reaches
divide sorrow from tears.
En route from false to true
you wither and grow dull.

We are amused by jets,
those crevices of silence
wedged between flight and sound:
"World record!" the world cheers.

But we've seen faster takeoffs:
their long-belated echo
still wrenches us from sleep
after so many years.

Outside, a storm of voices:
"We're innocent," they cry.
We rush to open windows,
lean out to catch their call.

But then the voices break off.
We watch the falling stars
just as after a salvo
plaster drops from the wall.

FUNERAL (I)

His skull, dug up from clay,
rests in a marble tomb;
sleep tight, medals, on pillows:
now it's got lots of room,
that skull dug up from clay.

They read off index cards:
a) he has been/will be missed,
b) go on, band, play the march,
c) too bad he can't see this.
They read off index cards.

Nation, be thankful now
for blessings you possess:
a being born just once
has two graves nonetheless.
Nation, be thankful now.

Parades were plentiful:
a thousand slide trombones,
police for crowd control,
bell-ringing for the bones.
Parades were plentiful.

Their eyes flicked heavenward
for omens from above:
a ray of light perhaps
or a bomb-carrying dove.
Their eyes flicked heavenward.

Between them and the people,
according to the plan,
the trees alone would sing
their silence on command.
Between them and the people.

Instead, bridges are drawn
above a gorge of stone,
its bed's been smoothed for tanks,
echoes await a moan.
Instead, bridges are drawn.

Still full of blood and hopes
the people turn away,
not knowing that bell ropes,
like human hair, turn gray.

Still full of blood and hopes.

BRUEGHEL'S TWO MONKEYS

This is what I see in my dreams about final exams:
two monkeys, chained to the floor, sit on the windowsill,
the sky behind them flutters,
the sea is taking its bath.

The exam is History of Mankind.
I stammer and hedge.

One monkey stares and listens with mocking disdain,
the other seems to be dreaming away—
but when it's clear I don't know what to say
he prompts me with a gentle
clinking of his chain.

STILL

Across the country's plains
sealed boxcars are carrying names:
how long will they travel, how far,
will they ever leave the boxcar—
don't ask, I can't say, I don't know.

The name Nathan beats the wall with his fist,
the name Isaac sings a mad hymn,
the name Aaron is dying of thirst,
the name Sarah begs water for him.

Don't jump from the boxcar, name David.
In these lands you're a name to avoid,
you're bound for defeat, you're a sign
pointing out those who must be destroyed.

At least give your son a Slavic name:
he'll need it. Here people count hairs
and examine the shape of your eyelids
to tell right from wrong, "ours" from "theirs."

Don't jump yet. Your son's name will be Lech.
Don't jump yet. The time's still not right.
Don't jump yet. The clattering wheels
are mocked by the echoes of night.

Clouds of people passed over this plain.
Vast clouds, but they held little rain—
just one tear, that's a fact, just one tear.
A dark forest. The tracks disappear.

That's-a-fact. The rail and the wheels.
That's-a-fact. A forest, no fields.
That's-a-fact. And their silence once more,
that's-a-fact, drums on my silent door.

ATLANTIS

They were or they weren't.
On an island or not.
An ocean or not an ocean
swallowed them up or it didn't.

Was there anyone to love anyone?
Did anybody have someone to fight?
Everything happened or it didn't
there or someplace else.

Seven cities stood there.
So we think.
They were meant to stand forever.
We suppose.

They weren't up to much, no.
They were up to something, yes.

Hypothetical. Dubious
Uncommemorated.
Never extracted from air,
fire, water, or earth.

Not contained within a stone
or drop of rain
Not suitable for straight-faced use
as a story's moral.

A meteor fell.
Not a meteor.
A volcano exploded.
Not a volcano.
Someone summoned something.
Nothing was called.

On this more-or-less Atlantis.

NOTES FROM A NONEXISTENT
HIMALAYAN EXPEDITION

So these are the Himalayas.
Mountains racing to the moon.
The moment of their start recorded
on the startling, ripped canvas of the sky.
Holes punched in a desert of clouds.
Thrust into nothing.
Echo—a white mute.
Quiet.

Yeti, down there we've got Wednesday,
bread and alphabets.
Two times two is four.
Roses are red there,
and violets are blue.

Yeti, crime is not all
we're up to down there.
Yeti, not every sentence there
means death.

We've inherited hope—
the gift of forgetting.
You'll see how we give
birth among the ruins.

Yeti, we've got Shakespeare there.
Yeti, we play solitaire
and violin. At nightfall,
we turn lights on, Yeti.

Up here it's neither moon nor earth.
Tears freeze.
Oh Yeti, semi-moonman,
turn back, think again!

I called this to the Yeti
inside four walls of avalanche,
stomping my feet for warmth
on the everlasting
snow.

NOTHING TWICE

Nothing can ever happen twice.
In consequence, the sorry fact is
that we arrive here improvised
and leave without the chance to practice.

Even if there is no one dumber,
if you're the planet's biggest dunce,
you can't repeat the class in summer:
this course is only offered once.

No day copies yesterday,
no two nights will teach what bliss is
in precisely the same way,
with exactly the same kisses.

One day, perhaps, some idle tongue
mentions your name by accident:
I feel as if a rose were flung
into the room, all hue and scent.

The next day, though you're here with me,
I can't help looking at the clock:
A rose? A rose? What could that be?
Is it a flower or a rock?

Why do we treat the fleeting day
with so much needless fear and sorrow?
It's in its nature not to stay:
Today is always gone tomorrow.

With smiles and kisses, we prefer
to seek accord beneath our star,
although we're different (we concur)
just as two drops of water are.

BUFFO

First, our love will die, alas,
then two hundred years will pass,
then we'll meet again at last—

this time in the theater, played
by a couple of comedians,
him and her, the public's darlings.

Just a little farce, with songs,
patter, jokes, and final bows,
a vaudeville comedy of manners,
certain to bring down the house.

You'll amuse them endlessly
on the stage with your cravat
and your petty jealousy.

So will I, love's silly pawn,
with my heart, my joy, my crown,
my heart broken, my joy gone,
my crown tumbling to the ground.

To the laughter's loud refrain,
we will meet and part again,
seven mountains, seven rivers
multiplying our pain.

If we haven't had enough
of despair, grief, all that stuff,
lofty words will kill us off.

Then we'll stand up, take our bows:
hope that you've enjoyed our show.
Every patron with his spouse
will applaud, get up, and go.

They'll reenter their lives' cages,
where love's tiger sometimes rages,
but the beast's too tame to bite.

We'll remain the odd ones out,
silly heathens in their fools' caps,
listening to the small bells ringing
day and night.

COMMEMORATION

They made love in a hazel grove,
beneath the little suns of dew;
dry leaves and twigs got in their hair
and dry dirt too.

Swallow's heart, have
mercy on them.

They both knelt down on the lakeshore,
they combed the dry leaves from their hair;
small fish, a star's converging rays,
swam up to stare.

Swallow's heart, have
mercy on them.

Reflected in the rippling lake,
trees trembled, nebulous and gray;
o swallow, let them never, never
forget this day.

O swallow, cloud-borne thorn,
anchor of the air,
Icarus improved,
coattails in Assumption,

o swallow, calligraphy,
clockhand minus minutes,
early ornithogothic,
heaven's cross-eyed glance,

o swallow, knife-edged silence,
mournful exuberance,
the aureole of lovers,
have mercy on them.

from

SALT

1962

THE MONKEY

Evicted from the Garden long before
the humans: he had such infectious eyes
that just one glance around old Paradise
made even angels' hearts feel sad and sore,
emotions hitherto unknown to them.
Without a chance to say "I disagree,"
he had to launch his earthly pedigree.
Today, still nimble, he retains his charme
with a primeval "e" after the "m."

Worshiped in Egypt, pleiades of fleas
spangling his sacred and silvery mane,
he'd sit and listen in archsilent peace:
What do you want? A life that never ends?
He'd turn his ruddy rump as if to say
such life he neither bans nor recommends.

In Europe they deprived him of his soul
but they forgot to take his hands away;
there was a painter-monk who dared portray
a saint with palms so thin, they could be simian.
The holy woman prayed for heaven's favor
as if she waited for a nut to fall.

Warm as a newborn, with an old man's tremor,
imported to kings' courts across the seas,
he whined while swinging on his golden chain,
dressed in the garish coat of a marquis.
Prophet of doom. The court is laughing? Please.

Considered edible in China, he makes boiled
or roasted faces when laid upon a salver.
Ironic as a gem set in sham gold.
His brain is famous for its subtle flavor,

though it's no good for trickier endeavors,
for instance, thinking up gunpowder.

In fables, lonely, not sure what to do,
he fills up mirrors with his indiscreet
self-mockery (a lesson for us, too);
the poor relation, who knows all about us,
though we don't greet each other when we meet.

LESSON

Subject King Alexander *predicate* cuts *direct*
object the Gordian knot with his *indirect object* sword.
This had never *predicate* entered anyone's *object* mind before.

None of a hundred philosophers could disentangle this knot.
No wonder each now shrinks in some secluded spot.
The soldiers, loud and with great glee,
grab each one by his trembling gray goatee
and *predicate* drag *object* him out.

Enough's enough. The king calls for his horse,
adjusts his crested helm and sallies forth.
And in his wake, with trumpets, drums, and flutes,
his *subject* army made of little knots
predicate marches off to *indirect object* war.

MUSEUM

Here are plates but no appetite.
And wedding rings, but the requited love
has been gone now for some three hundred years.

Here's a fan—where is the maiden's blush?
Here are swords—where is the ire?
Nor will the lute sound at the twilight hour.

Since eternity was out of stock,
ten thousand aging things have been amassed instead.
The moss-grown guard in golden slumber
props his moustache on the Exhibit Number . . .

Eight. Metals, clay, and feathers celebrate
their silent triumphs over dates.
Only some Egyptian flapper's silly hairpin giggles.

The crown has outlasted the head.
The hand has lost out to the glove.
The right shoe has defeated the foot.

As for me, I am still alive, you see.
The battle with my dress still rages on.
It struggles, foolish thing, so stubbornly!
Determined to keep living when I'm gone!

A MOMENT IN TROY

Little girls—
skinny, resigned
to freckles that won't go away,

not turning any heads
as they walk across the eyelids of the world,

looking just like Mom or Dad,
and sincerely horrified by it—

in the middle of dinner,
in the middle of a book,
while studying the mirror,
may suddenly be taken off to Troy.

In the grand boudoir of a wink
they all turn into beautiful Helens.

They ascend the royal staircase
in the rustling of silk and admiration.
They feel light. They all know
that beauty equals rest,
that lips mold the speech's meaning,
and gestures sculpt themselves
in inspired nonchalance.

Their small faces
worth dismissing envoys for
extend proudly on necks
that merit countless sieges.

Those tall, dark movie stars,
their girlfriends' older brothers,
the teacher from art class,
alas, they must all be slain.

Little girls
observe disaster
from a tower of smiles.

Little girls
wring their hands
in intoxicating mock despair.

Little girls
against a backdrop of destruction,
with flaming towns for tiaras,
in earrings of pandemic lamentation.

Pale and tearless.
Triumphant. Sated with the view.
Dreading only the inevitable
moment of return.

Little girls
returning.

SHADOW

My shadow is a fool whose feelings
are often hurt by his routine
of rising up behind his queen
to bump his silly head on ceilings.

His is a world of two dimensions,
that's true, but flat jokes still can smart;
he longs to flaunt my court's conventions
and drop a role he knows by heart.

The queen leans out above the sill,
the jester tumbles out for real:
thus they divide their actions; still,
it's not a fifty-fifty deal.

My jester took on nothing less
than royal gestures' shamelessness,
the things that I'm too weak to bear—
the cloak, crown, scepter, and the rest.

I'll stay serene, won't feel a thing,
yes, I will turn my head away
after I say good-bye, my king,
at railway station N., some day.

My king, it is the fool who'll lie
across the tracks; the fool, not I.

THE REST

Her mad songs over, Ophelia darts out,
anxious to check offstage whether her dress is
still not too crumpled, whether her blond tresses
frame her face as they should.

                          Since real life's laws
require facts, she, Polonius's true
daughter, carefully washes black despair
out of her eyebrows, and is not above
counting the leaves she's combed out of her hair.
Oh, may Denmark forgive you, my dear, and me too:
I'll die with wings, I'll live on with practical claws.
Non omnis moriar of love.

CLOCHARD

In Paris, on a day that stayed morning until dusk,
in a Paris like—
in a Paris which—
(save me, sacred folly of description!)
in a garden by a stone cathedral
(not built, no, rather
played upon a lute)
a *clochard,* a lay monk, a naysayer
sleeps sprawled like a knight in effigy.

If he ever owned anything, he has lost it,
and having lost it doesn't want it back.
He's still owed soldier's pay for the conquest of Gaul—
but he's got over that, it doesn't matter.
And they never paid him in the fifteenth century
for posing as the thief on Christ's left hand—
he has forgotten all about it, he's not waiting.

He earns his red wine
by trimming the neighborhood dogs.
He sleeps with the air of an inventor of dreams,
his thick beard swarming toward the sun.

The gray chimeras (to wit, bulldogryphons,
hellephants, hippopotoads, croakodilloes, rhinocerberuses,
behemammoths, and demonopods,
that omnibestial Gothic *allegro vivace*)
unpetrify

and examine him with a curiosity
they never turn on me or you,
prudent Peter,
zealous Michael,
enterprising Eve,
Barbara, Clare.

"*La Pologne? La Pologne?* Isn't it terribly cold there?" she asked, and then sighed with relief. So many countries have been turning up lately that the safest thing to talk about is climate.

"Madame," I want to reply, "my people's poets do all their writing in mittens. I don't mean to imply that they never remove them; they do, indeed, if the moon is warm enough. In stanzas composed of raucous whooping, for only such can drown the windstorms' constant roar, they glorify the simple lives of our walrus herders. Our Classicists engrave their odes with inky icicles on trampled snowdrifts. The rest, our Decadents, bewail their fate with snowflakes instead of tears. He who wishes to drown himself must have an ax at hand to cut the ice. Oh, madame, dearest madame."

That's what I mean to say. But I've forgotten the word for walrus in French. And I'm not sure of icicle and ax.

"*La Pologne? La Pologne?* Isn't it terribly cold there?"

"*Pas du tout,*" I answer icily.

TRAVEL ELEGY

Everything's mine but just on loan,
nothing for the memory to hold,
though mine as long as I look.

Memories come to mind like excavated statues
that have misplaced their heads.

From the town of Samokov, only rain
and more rain.

Paris from Louvre to fingernail
grows web-eyed by the moment.

Boulevard Saint-Martin: some stairs
leading into a fade-out.

Only a bridge and a half
from Leningrad of the bridges.

Poor Uppsala, reduced to a splinter
of its mighty cathedral.

Sofia's hapless dancer,
a form without a face.

Then separately, his face without eyes;
separately again, eyes with no pupils,
and, finally, the pupils of a cat.

A Caucasian eagle soars
above a reproduction of a canyon,
the fool's gold of the sun,
the phony stones.

Everything's mine but just on loan,
nothing for the memory to hold,
though mine as long as I look.

Inexhaustible, unembraceable,
but particular to the smallest fiber,
grain of sand, drop of water—
landscapes.

I won't retain one blade of grass
as it's truly seen.

Salutation and farewell
in a single glance.

For surplus and absence alike,
a single motion of the neck.

WITHOUT A TITLE

The two of them were left so long alone,
so much in un-love, without a word to spare,
what they deserve by now is probably
a miracle—a thunderbolt, or turning into stone.
Two million books in print on Greek mythology,
but there's no rescue in them for this pair.

If at least someone would ring the bell, or if
something would flare and disappear again,
no matter from where and no matter when,
no matter if it's fun, fear, joy, or grief.

But nothing of the sort. No aberration,
no deviation from the well-made plot
this bourgeois drama holds. There'll be a dot
above the "i" inside their tidy separation.

Against the backdrop of the steadfast wall,
pitying one another, they both stare
into the mirror, but there's nothing there
except their sensible reflections. All

they see is the two people in the frame.
Matter is on alert. All its dimensions,
everything in between the ground and sky
keeps close watch on the fates that we were born with
and sees to it that they remain the same—
although we still don't see the reason why
a sudden deer bounding across this room
would shatter the entire universe.

AN UNEXPECTED MEETING

We treat each other with exceeding courtesy;
we say, it's great to see you after all these years.

Our tigers drink milk.
Our hawks tread the ground.
Our sharks have all drowned.
Our wolves yawn beyond the open cage.

Our snakes have shed their lightning,
our apes their flights of fancy,
our peacocks have renounced their plumes.
The bats flew out of our hair long ago.

We fall silent in midsentence,
all smiles, past help.
Our humans
don't know how to talk to one another.

GOLDEN ANNIVERSARY

They must have been different once,
fire and water, miles apart,
robbing and giving in desire,
that assault on one another's otherness.
Embracing, they appropriated and expropriated each other
for so long,
that only air was left within their arms,
transparent as if after lightning.

One day the answer came before the question.
Another night they guessed their eyes' expression
by the type of silence in the dark.

Gender fades, mysteries molder,
distinctions meet in all-resemblance
just as all colors coincide in white.

Which of them is doubled and which missing?
Which one is smiling with two smiles?
Whose voice forms a two-part canon?
When both heads nod, which one agrees?
Whose gesture lifts the teaspoon to their lips?
Who's flayed the other one alive?
Which one lives and which has died
entangled in the lines of whose palm?

They gazed into each other's eyes and slowly twins emerged.
Familiarity breeds the most perfect of mothers—
it favors neither of the little darlings,
it scarcely can recall which one is which.

On this festive day, their golden anniversary,
a dove, seen identically, perched on the windowsill.

Write it down. Write it. With ordinary ink
on ordinary paper: they weren't given food,
they all died of hunger. *All. How many?*
It's a large meadow. How much grass
per head? Write down: I don't know.
History rounds off skeletons to zero.
A thousand and one is still only a thousand.
That *one* seems never to have existed:
a fictitious fetus, an empty cradle,
a primer opened for no one,
air that laughs, cries, and grows,
stairs for a void bounding out to the garden,
no one's spot in the ranks.

It became flesh right here, on this meadow.
But the meadow's silent, like a witness who's been bought.
Sunny. Green. A forest close at hand,
with wood to chew on, drops beneath the bark to drink—
a view served round the clock,
until you go blind. Above, a bird
whose shadow flicked its nourishing wings
across their lips. Jaws dropped,
teeth clattered.

At night a sickle glistened in the sky
and reaped the dark for dreamed-of loaves.
Hands came flying from blackened icons,
each holding an empty chalice.
A man swayed
on a grill of barbed wire.
Some sang, with dirt in their mouths. *That lovely song*
about war hitting you straight in the heart.
Write how quiet it is.
Yes.

PARABLE

Some fishermen pulled a bottle from the deep. It held a piece of paper, with these words: "Somebody save me! I'm here. The ocean cast me on this desert island. I am standing on the shore waiting for help. Hurry! I'm here!"

"There's no date. I bet it's already too late anyway. It could have been floating for years," the first fisherman said.

"And he doesn't say where. It's not even clear which ocean," the second fisherman said.

"It's not too late, or too far. The island Here is everywhere," the third fisherman said.

They all felt awkward. No one spoke. That's how it goes with universal truths.

BALLAD

Hear the ballad "Murdered Woman
Suddenly Gets Up from Chair."

It's an honest ballad, penned
neither to shock nor offend.

The thing happened fair and square,
with curtains open, lamps all lit:

passersby could stop and stare.

When the door had shut behind him
and the killer ran downstairs,
she stood up, just like the living
startled by the sudden silence.

She gets up, she moves her head,
and she looks around with eyes
harder than they were before.

No, she doesn't float through air:
she steps on the ordinary,
wooden, slightly creaky floor.

In the oven she burns traces
that the killer's left behind:
here a picture, there shoelaces,
everything that she can find.

It's obvious that she's not strangled.
It's obvious that she's not shot.
She's been killed invisibly.

She may still show signs of life,
cry for sundry silly reasons,
shriek in horror at the sight
of a mouse.
            Ridiculous

traits are so predictable
that they aren't hard to fake.

She got up like you and me.

She walks just as people do.

And she sings and combs her hair,
which still grows.

OVER WINE

He glanced, gave me extra charm
and I took it as my own.
Happily I gulped a star.

I let myself be invented,
modeled on my own reflection
in his eyes. I dance, dance, dance
in the stir of sudden wings.

The chair's a chair, the wine is wine,
in a wineglass that's the wineglass
standing there by standing there.
Only I'm imaginary,
make-believe beyond belief,
so fictitious that it hurts.

And I tell him tales about
ants that die of love beneath
a dandelion's constellation.
I swear a white rose will sing
if you sprinkle it with wine.

I laugh and I tilt my head
cautiously, as if to check
whether the invention works.
I dance, dance inside my stunned
skin, in his arms that create me.

Eve from the rib, Venus from foam,
Minerva from Jupiter's head—
all three were more real than me.

When he isn't looking at me,
I try to catch my reflection
on the wall. And see the nail
where a picture used to be.

RUBENS' WOMEN

Titanettes, female fauna,
naked as the rumbling of barrels.
They roost in trampled beds,
asleep, with mouths agape, ready to crow.
Their pupils have fled into flesh
and sound the glandular depths
from which yeast seeps into their blood.

Daughters of the Baroque. Dough
thickens in troughs, baths steam, wines blush,
cloudy piglets career across the sky,
triumphant trumpets neigh the carnal alarm.

O pumpkin plump! O pumped-up corpulence
inflated double by disrobing
and tripled by your tumultuous poses!
O fatty dishes of love!

Their skinny sisters woke up earlier,
before dawn broke and shone upon the painting.
And no one saw how they went single file
along the canvas's unpainted side.

Exiled by style. Only their ribs stood out.
With birdlike feet and palms, they strove
to take wing on their jutting shoulder blades.

The thirteenth century would have given them golden haloes.
The twentieth, silver screens.
The seventeenth, alas, holds nothing for the unvoluptuous.

For even the sky bulges here
with pudgy angels and a chubby god—
thick-whiskered Phoebus, on a sweaty steed,
riding straight into the seething bedchamber.

COLORATURA

Poised beneath a twig-wigged tree,
she spills her sparkling vocal powder:
slippery sound slivers, silvery
like spider's spittle, only louder.

Oh yes, she Cares (with a high C)
for Fellow Humans (you and me);
for us she'll twitter nothing bitter;
she'll knit her fitter, sweeter glitter;
her vocal cords mince words for us
and crumble croutons, with crisp crunch
(lunch for her little lambs to munch)
into a cream-filled demitasse.

But hark! It's dark! Oh doom too soon!
She's threatened by the black bassoon!
It's hoarse and coarse, it's grim and gruff,
it calls her dainty voice's bluff—
Basso Profundo, end this terror,
do-re-mi mene tekel et cetera!

You want to silence her, abduct her
to our chilly life behind the scenes?
To our Siberian steppes of stopped-up sinuses,
frogs in all throats, eternal hems and haws,
where we, poor souls, gape soundlessly
like fish? And this is what you wish?

Oh nay! Oh nay! Though doom be nigh,
she'll keep her chin and pitch up high!
Her fate is hanging by a hair
of voice so thin it sounds like *air*,
but that's enough for her to take
a breath and soar, without a break,

chandelierward; and while she's there,
her vox humana crystal-clears
the whole world up. And we're all ears.

BODYBUILDERS' CONTEST

From scalp to sole, all muscles in slow motion.
The ocean of his torso drips with lotion.
The king of all is he who preens and wrestles
with sinews twisted into monstrous pretzels.

Onstage, he grapples with a grizzly bear
the deadlier for not really being there.
Three unseen panthers are in turn laid low,
each with one smoothly choreographed blow.

He grunts while showing his poses and paces.
His back alone has twenty different faces.
The mammoth fist he raises as he wins
is tribute to the force of vitamins.

POETRY READING

To be a boxer, or not to be there
at all. O Muse, where are *our* teeming crowds?
Twelve people in the room, eight seats to spare—
it's time to start this cultural affair.
Half came inside because it started raining,
the rest are relatives. O Muse.

The women here would love to rant and rave,
but that's for boxing. Here they must behave.
Dante's Inferno is ringside nowadays.
Likewise his Paradise. O Muse.

Oh, not to be a boxer but a poet,
one sentenced to hard shelleying for life,
for lack of muscles forced to show the world
the sonnet that may make the high-school reading lists
with luck. O Muse,
O bobtailed angel, Pegasus.

In the first row, a sweet old man's soft snore:
he dreams his wife's alive again. What's more,
she's making him that tart she used to bake.
Aflame, but carefully—don't burn his cake!—
we start to read. O Muse.

EPITAPH

Here lies, old-fashioned as parentheses,
the authoress of verse. Eternal rest
was granted her by earth, although the corpse
had failed to join the avant-garde, of course.
The plain grave? There's poetic justice in it,
this ditty-dirge, the owl, the burdock. Passerby,
take out your compact Compu-Brain and try
to weigh Szymborska's fate for half a minute.

PROLOGUE TO A COMEDY

He made himself a glass violin so he could see what music looks like. He dragged his boat to the mountain's peak and waited for the sea to reach his level. At night, he got engrossed in railway schedules: the terminals moved him to tears. He grew rozes with a "z." He wrote one poem to cure baldness, and another on the same subject. He broke the clock at City Hall to stop the leaves from falling once and for all. He planned to excavate a city in a pot of chives. He walked with the globe chained to his leg, very slowly, smiling, happy as two times two is two. When they said he didn't exist, he couldn't die of grief, so he had to be born. He's already out there living somewhere; he blinks his little eyes and grows. Just in time! The very nick of time! Our Most Gracious Lady, Our Wise and Sweet Lady Machine will soon have need of a fool like this for her fit amusement and innocent pleasure.

LIKENESS

If the gods' favorites die young—
what to do with the rest of your life?
Old age is a precipice,
that is, if youth is a peak.

I won't budge.
I'll stay young if I have to do it on one leg.
I'll latch onto the air
with whiskers thin as a mouse's squeak.
In this posture I'll be born over and over.
It's the only art I know.

But these things will always be me:
the magic gloves,
the boutonniere left from my first masquerade,
the falsetto of youthful manifestos,
the face straight from a seamstress's dream about a croupier,
the eyes I loved to pluck out in my paintings
and scatter like peas from a pod,
because at that sight a twitch ran through the dead thighs
of the public frog.

Be amazed, you too.
Be amazed: for all of Diogenes' tubs,
I still beat him as conceptualist.
Pray
for your eternal test.
What I hold in my hands
are the spiders that I dip in Chinese ink
and fling against the canvas.
I enter the world once more.
A new navel blooms
on the artist's belly.

I AM TOO CLOSE . . .

I am too close for him to dream of me.
I don't flutter over him, don't flee him
beneath the roots of trees. I am too close.
The caught fish doesn't sing with my voice.
The ring doesn't roll from my finger.
I am too close. The great house is on fire
without me calling for help. Too close
for one of my hairs to turn into the rope
of the alarm bell. Too close to enter
as the guest before whom walls retreat.
I'll never die again so lightly,
so far beyond my body, so unknowingly
as I did once in his dream. I am too close,
too close. I hear the word hiss
and see its glistening scales as I lie motionless
in his embrace. He's sleeping,
more accessible at this moment to an usherette
he saw once in a traveling circus with one lion,
than to me, who lies at his side.
A valley now grows within him for her,
rusty-leaved, with a snowcapped mountain at one end
rising in the azure air. I am too close
to fall from that sky like a gift from heaven.
My cry could only waken him. And what
a poor gift: I, confined to my own form,
when I used to be a birch, a lizard
shedding times and satin skins
in many shimmering hues. And I possessed
the gift of vanishing before astonished eyes,
which is the richest of all. I am too close,
too close for him to dream of me.

I slip my arm from underneath his sleeping head—
it's numb, swarming with imaginary pins.
A host of fallen angels perches on each tip,
waiting to be counted.

THE TOWER OF BABEL

"What time is it?" "Oh yes, I'm so happy;
all I need is a little bell round my neck
to jingle over you while you're asleep."
"Didn't you hear the storm? The north wind shook
the walls; the tower gate, like a lion's maw,
yawned on its creaking hinges." "How could you
forget? I had on that plain gray dress
that fastens on the shoulder." *"At that moment,*
myriad explosions shook the sky." "How could I
come in? You weren't alone, after all." *"I glimpsed*
colors older than sight itself." "Too bad
you can't promise me." *"You're right, it must have been*
a dream." "Why all these lies; why do you call me
by her name; do you still love her?" *"Of course,*
I want you to stay with me." "I can't
complain. I should have guessed myself."
"Do you still think about him?" "But I'm not crying."
"That's all there is?" "No one but you."
"At least you're honest." "Don't worry,
I'm leaving town." *"Don't worry,*
I'm going." "You have such beautiful hands."
"That's ancient history; the blade went through
but missed the bone." "Never mind, darling,
never mind." *"I don't know*
what time it is, and I don't care."

WATER

A drop of water fell on my hand,
drawn from the Ganges and the Nile,

from hoarfrost ascended to heaven off a seal's whiskers,
from jugs broken in the cities of Ys and Tyre.

On my index finger
the Caspian Sea isn't landlocked,

and the Pacific is the Rudawa's meek tributary,
the same stream that floated in a little cloud over Paris

in the year seven hundred and sixty-four
on the seventh of May at three a.m.

There are not enough mouths to utter
all your fleeting names, O water.

I would have to name you in every tongue,
pronouncing all the vowels at once

while also keeping silent—for the sake of the lake
that still goes unnamed

and doesn't exist on this earth, just as the star
reflected in it is not in the sky.

Someone was drowning, someone dying was
calling out for you. Long ago, yesterday.

You have saved houses from fire, you have carried off
houses and trees, forests and towns alike.

You've been in christening fonts and courtesans' baths.
In coffins and kisses.

Gnawing at stone, feeding rainbows.
In the sweat and the dew of pyramids and lilacs.

How light the raindrop's contents are.
How gently the world touches me.

Whenever wherever whatever has happened
is written on waters of Babel.

Job, sorely tried in both flesh and possessions, curses man's fate. It is great poetry. His friends arrive and, rending their garments, dissect Job's guilt before the Lord. Job cries out that he was righteous. Job does not know why the Lord smote him. Job does not want to talk to them. Job wants to talk to the Lord. The Lord God appears in a chariot of whirlwinds. Before him who had been cloven to the bone, He praises the work of His hands: the heavens, the seas, the earth and the beasts thereon. Especially Behemoth, and Leviathan in particular, creatures of which the Deity is justly proud. It is great poetry. Job listens: the Lord God beats around the bush, for the Lord God wishes to beat around the bush. Job therefore hastily prostrates himself before the Lord. Events now transpire in rapid succession. Job regains his donkeys and camels, his oxen and sheep twofold. Skin grows over his grinning skull. And Job goes along with it. Job agrees. Job does not want to ruin a masterpiece.

IN HERACLITUS'S RIVER

In Heraclitus's river
a fish is busy fishing,
a fish guts a fish with a sharp fish,
a fish builds a fish, a fish lives in a fish,
a fish escapes from a fish under siege.

In Heraclitus's river
a fish loves a fish,
your eyes, it says, glow like the fishes in the sky,
I would swim at your side to the sea we will share,
o fairest of the shoal.

In Heraclitus's river
a fish has imagined the fish of all fish,
a fish kneels to the fish, a fish sings to the fish,
a fish begs the fish to ease its fishy lot.

In Heraclitus's river
I, the solitary fish, a fish apart
(apart at least from the tree fish and the stone fish),
write, at isolated moments, a tiny fish or two
whose glittering scales, so fleeting,
may only be the dark's embarrassed wink.

CONVERSATION WITH A STONE

I knock at the stone's front door.
"It's only me, let me come in.
I want to enter your insides,
have a look round,
breathe my fill of you."

"Go away," says the stone.
"I'm shut tight.
Even if you break me to pieces,
we'll all still be closed.
You can grind us to sand,
we still won't let you in."

I knock at the stone's front door.
"It's only me, let me come in.
I've come out of pure curiosity.
Only life can quench it.
I mean to stroll through your palace,
then go calling on a leaf, a drop of water.
I don't have much time.
My mortality should touch you."

"I'm made of stone," says the stone,
"and must therefore keep a straight face.
Go away.
I don't have the muscles to laugh."

I knock at the stone's front door.
"It's only me, let me come in.
I hear you have great empty halls inside you,
unseen, their beauty in vain,
soundless, not echoing anyone's steps.
Admit you don't know them well yourself."

"Great and empty, true enough," says the stone,
"but there isn't any room.
Beautiful, perhaps, but not to the taste
of your poor senses.
You may get to know me, but you'll never know me through.
My whole surface is turned toward you,
all my insides turned away."

I knock at the stone's front door.
"It's only me, let me come in.
I don't seek refuge for eternity.
I'm not unhappy.
I'm not homeless.
My world is worth returning to.
I'll enter and exit empty-handed.
And my proof I was there
will be only words,
which no one will believe."

"You shall not enter," says the stone.
"You lack the sense of taking part.
No other sense can make up for your missing sense of taking part.
Even sight heightened to become all-seeing
will do you no good without a sense of taking part.
You shall not enter, you have only a sense of what that sense
    should be,
only its seed, imagination."

I knock at the stone's front door.
"It's only me, let me come in.
I haven't got two thousand centuries,
so let me come under your roof."

"If you don't believe me," says the stone,
"just ask the leaf, it will tell you the same.

Ask a drop of water, it will say what the leaf has said.
And, finally, ask a hair from your own head.
I am bursting with laughter, yes, laughter, vast laughter,
although I don't know how to laugh."

I knock at the stone's front door.
"It's only me, let me come in."

"I don't have a door," says the stone.

NO END OF FUN

1967

THE JOY OF WRITING

Why does this written doe bound through these written woods?
For a drink of written water from a spring
whose surface will xerox her soft muzzle?
Why does she lift her head; does she hear something?
Perched on four slim legs borrowed from the truth,
she pricks up her ears beneath my fingertips.
Silence—this word also rustles across the page
and parts the boughs
that have sprouted from the word "woods."

Lying in wait, set to pounce on the blank page,
are letters up to no good,
clutches of clauses so subordinate
they'll never let her get away.

Each drop of ink contains a fair supply
of hunters, equipped with squinting eyes behind their sights,
prepared to swarm the sloping pen at any moment,
surround the doe, and slowly aim their guns.

They forget that what's here isn't life.
Other laws, black on white, obtain.
The twinkling of an eye will take as long as I say,
and will, if I wish, divide into tiny eternities,
full of bullets stopped in mid-flight.
Not a thing will ever happen unless I say so.
Without my blessing, not a leaf will fall,
not a blade of grass will bend beneath that little hoof's full stop.

Is there then a world
where I rule absolutely on fate?
A time I bind with chains of signs?
An existence become endless at my bidding?

The joy of writing.
The power of preserving.
Revenge of a mortal hand.

MEMORY FINALLY

Memory's finally found what it was after.
My mother has turned up, my father has been spotted.
I dreamed up a table and two chairs. They sat.
They were mine again, alive again for me.
The two lamps of their faces gleamed at dusk
as if for Rembrandt.

Only now can I begin to tell
in how many dreams they've wandered, in how many crowds
I dragged them out from underneath the wheels,
in how many deathbeds they moaned with me at their side.
Cut off, they grew back, but never straight.
The absurdity drove them to disguises.
So what if they felt no pain outside me,
they still ached within me.
In my dreams, gawking crowds heard me call out Mom
to a bouncing, chirping thing up on a branch.
They made fun of my father's hair in pigtails.
I woke up ashamed.

So, finally.
One ordinary Friday night
they suddenly came back
exactly as I wanted.
In a dream, but somehow freed from dreams,
obeying just themselves and nothing else.
In the picture's background possibilities grew dim,
accidents lacked the necessary shape.
Only they shone, beautiful because just like themselves.
They appeared to me for a long, long, happy time.

I woke up. I opened my eyes.
I touched the world, a chiseled picture-frame.

LANDSCAPE

In the old master's landscape,
the trees have roots beneath the oil paint,
the path undoubtedly reaches its goal,
the signature is replaced by a stately blade of grass,
it's a persuasive five in the afternoon,
May has been gently, yet firmly, detained,
so I've lingered, too. Why, of course, my dear,
I am the woman there, under the ash tree.

Just see how far behind I've left you,
see the white bonnet and the yellow skirt I wear,
see how I grip my basket so as not to slip out of the painting,
how I strut within another's fate
and rest awhile from living mysteries.

Even if you called I wouldn't hear you,
and even if I heard I wouldn't turn,
and even if I made that impossible gesture
your face would seem a stranger's face to me.

I know the world six miles around.
I know the herbs and spells for every pain.
God still looks down on the crown of my head.
I still pray I won't die suddenly.
War is punishment and peace is a reward.
Shameful dreams all come from Satan.
My soul is as plain as the stone of a plum.

I don't know the games of the heart.
I've never seen my children's father naked.
I don't see the crabbed and blotted draft
that hides behind the Song of Songs.
What I want to say comes in ready-made phrases.
I never use despair, since it isn't really mine,
only given to me for safekeeping.

Even if you bar my way,
even if you stare me in the face,
I'll pass you by on the chasm's edge, finer than a hair.

On the right is my house. I know it from all sides,
along with its steps and its entryway,
behind which life goes on unpainted.
The cat hops on a bench,
the sun gleams on a pewter jug,
a bony man sits at the table
fixing a clock.

FAMILY ALBUM

No one in this family has ever died of love.
No food for myth and nothing magisterial.
Consumptive Romeos? Juliets diphtherial?
A doddering second childhood was enough.
No death-defying vigils, love-struck poses
over unrequited letters strewn with tears!
Here, in conclusion, as scheduled, appears
a portly, pince-nez'd neighbor bearing roses.
No suffocation-in-the-closet gaffes
because the cuckold returned home too early!
Those frills or furbelows, however flounced and whirly,
barred no one from the family photographs.
No Bosch-like hell within their souls, no wretches
found bleeding in the garden, shirts in stains!
(True, some did die with bullets in their brains,
for other reasons, though, and on field stretchers.)
Even this belle with rapturous coiffure
who may have danced till dawn—but nothing smarter—
hemorrhaged to a better world, *bien sûr,*
but not to taunt or hurt *you,* slick-haired partner.
For others, Death was mad and monumental—
not for these citizens of a sepia past.
Their griefs turned into smiles, their days flew fast,
their vanishing was due to influenza.

LAUGHTER

The little girl I was—
I know her, of course.
I have a few snapshots
from her brief life.
I feel good-natured pity
for a couple of little poems.
I remember a few events.

But
to make the man who's with me
laugh and hug me,
I dig up just one silly story:
the puppy love
of that ugly duckling.

I tell him
how she fell in love with a college boy;
that is, she wanted him
to look at her.

I tell him
how she once ran out to meet him
with a bandage on her unhurt head,
so that he'd ask, oh just ask her
what had happened.

Funny little thing.
How could she know
that even despair can work for you
if you're lucky enough
to outlive it.

I'd give her some change: go buy a cookie.
I'd give her more: go see a show.
Go away, I'm busy now.

Can't you see
the lights are out?
Don't you get it,
the door is locked?
Stop fiddling with the knob—
the man who laughed
and hugged me
is not your college boy.

It'd be better if you
went back where you came from.
I don't owe you anything,
I'm just an ordinary woman
who only knows
when to betray
another's secret.

Don't keep staring at us
with those eyes of yours,
open too wide
like the eyes of the dead.

THE RAILROAD STATION

My nonarrival in the city of N.
took place on the dot.

You'd been alerted
in my unmailed letter.

You were able not to be there
at the agreed-upon time.

The train pulled up at Platform 3.
A lot of people got out.

My absence joined the throng
as it made its way toward the exit.

Several women rushed
to take my place
in all that rush.

Somebody ran up to one of them.
I didn't know him,
but she recognized him
immediately.

While they kissed
with not our lips,
a suitcase disappeared,
not mine.

The railroad station in the city of N.
passed its exam
in objective existence
with flying colors.

The whole remained in place.
Particulars scurried
along the designated tracks.

Even a rendezvous
took place as planned.

Beyond the reach
of our presence.

In the paradise lost
of probability.

Somewhere else.
Somewhere else.
How these little words ring.

ALIVE

These days we just hold him.
Hold him living.
Only the heart
still pounces on him.

To the dismay
of our distaff cousin, the spider,
he will not be devoured.

We permit his head,
pardoned centuries ago,
to rest upon our shoulder.

For a thousand tangled reasons
it's become our practice
to listen to him breathe.

Hissed from our mysteries.
Broken of our bloody ways.
Stripped of female menace.

Only the fingernails
still glitter, scratch, and retract.
Do they know,
can they guess
that they're the last set of silverware
from the family fortune?

He's already forgotten
he should flee us.
He doesn't know the wide-eyed fear
that grabs you by the short hairs.

He looks as if
he'd just been born.
All out of us.
All ours.

On his cheek,
an eyelash's imploring shadow.
Between his shoulderblades,
a touching trickle of sweat.

That's what he is now,
and that's how he'll nod off.
Truthful.
Hugged by a death
whose permit has elapsed.

BORN

So this is his mother.
This small woman.
The gray-eyed procreator.

The boat in which, years ago,
he sailed to shore.

The boat from which he stepped
into the world,
into un-eternity.

Genetrix of the man
with whom I leap through fire.

So this is she, the only one
who didn't take him
finished and complete.

She herself pulled him
into the skin I know,
bound him to the bones
that are hidden from me.

She herself raised
the gray eyes
that he raised to me.

So this is she, his Alpha.
Why has he shown her to me.

Born
So he was born, too.
Born like everyone else.
Like me, who will die.

The son of an actual woman.
A new arrival from the body's depths.
A voyager to Omega.

Subject to
his own absence,
on every front,
at any moment.

He hits his head
against a wall
that won't give way forever.

His movements
dodge and parry
the universal verdict.

I realized
that his journey was already halfway over.

But he didn't tell me that,
no.

"This is my mother."
was all he said.

CENSUS

On the hill where Troy once stood,
they've dug up seven cities.
Seven cities. Six too many
for a single epic.
What's to be done with them? What?
Hexameters burst,
nonfictional bricks appear between the cracks,
ruined walls rise mutely as in silent films,
charred beams, broken chains,
bottomless pitchers drained dry,
fertility charms, olive pits,
and skulls as palpable as tomorrow's moon.

Our stockpile of antiquity grows constantly,
it's overflowing,
reckless squatters jostle for a place in history,
hordes of sword fodder,
Hector's nameless extras, no less brave than he,
thousands upon thousands of singular faces,
each the first and last for all time,
in each a pair of inimitable eyes.
How easy it was to live not knowing this,
so sentimental, so spacious.

What should we give them? What do they need?
Some more or less unpeopled century?
Some small appreciation for their goldsmiths' art?
We three billion judges
have problems of our own,
our own inarticulate rabble,
railroad stations, bleachers, protests and processions,
vast numbers of remote streets, floors, and walls.

We pass each other once for all time in department stores
shopping for a new pitcher.
Homer is working in the census bureau.
No one knows what he does in his spare time.

SOLILOQUY FOR CASSANDRA

Here I am, Cassandra.
And this is my city under ashes.
And these are my prophet's staff and ribbons.
And this is my head full of doubts.

It's true, I am triumphant.
My prophetic words burn like fire in the sky.
Only unacknowledged prophets
are privy to such prospects.
Only those who got off on the wrong foot,
whose predictions turned to fact so quickly—
it's as if they'd never lived.

I remember it so clearly—
how people, seeing me, would break off in midword.
Laughter died.
Lovers' hands unclasped.
Children ran to their mothers.
I didn't even know their short lived names.
And that song about a little green leaf—
no one ever finished it near me.

I loved them.
But I loved them haughtily.
From heights beyond life.
From the future. Where it's always empty
and nothing is easier than seeing death.
I'm sorry that my voice was hard.
Look down on yourselves from the stars, I cried,
look down on yourselves from the stars.
They heard me and lowered their eyes.

They lived within life.
Pierced by that great wind.

Condemned.
Trapped from birth in departing bodies.
But in them they bore a moist hope,
a flame fuelled by its own flickering.
They really knew what a moment means,
oh any moment, any one at all
before—

It turns out I was right.
But nothing has come of it.
And this is my robe, slightly singed.
And this is my prophet's junk.
And this is my twisted face.
A face that didn't know it could be beautiful.

A BYZANTINE MOSAIC

"O Theotropia, my empress consort."

"O Theodendron, my consort emperor."

"How fair thou art, my hollow-cheeked beloved."

"How fine art thou, blue-lipped spouse."

"Thou art so wondrous frail
beneath thy bell-like gown,
the alarum of which, if but removed,
would waken all my kingdom."

"How excellently mortified thou art,
my lord and master,
to mine own shadow a twinnèd shade."

"Oh how it pleaseth me
to see my lady's palms,
like unto palm leaves verily,
clasped to her mantle's throat."

"Wherewith, raised heavenward,
I would pray thee mercy for our son,
for he is not such as we, O Theodendron."

"Heaven forfend, O Theotropia.
Pray, what might he be,
begotten and brought forth
in godly dignity?"

"I will confess anon, and thou shalt hear me.
Not a princeling but a sinner have I borne thee.
Pink and shameless as a piglet,
plump and merry, verily,
all chubby wrists and ringlets came he
rolling unto us."

"He is roly-poly?"

"That he is."

"He is voracious?"

"Yea, in truth."

"His skin is milk and roses?"

"As thou sayest."

"What, pray, does our archimandrite say,
a man of most penetrating gnosis?
What say our consecrated eremites,
most holy skeletesses?
How should they strip the fiendish infant
of his swaddling silks?"

"Metamorphosis miraculous
still lies within our Savior's power.
Yet thou, on spying
the babe's unsightliness,
shalt not cry out
and rouse the sleeping demon from his rest?"

"I am thy twin in horror.
Lead on, Theotropia."

BEHEADING

Décolletage comes from *decollo,*
decollo means I cut off at the neck.
The Queen of Scots, Mary Stuart,
ascended the scaffold in an appropriate shift.
The shift was *décolleté*
and red as a hemorrhage.

At that very moment,
in a secluded chamber,
Elizabeth Tudor, Queen of England,
stood at the window in a white dress.
The dress was triumphantly fastened to the chin
and finished in a starched ruff.

They thought in unison:
"Lord, have mercy on me"
"Right is on my side"
"Living means getting in the way"
"Under certain circumstances the owl is the baker's daughter"
"This will never end"
"It is already over"
"What am I doing here, there's nothing here"

The difference in dress—yes, this we know for sure.
The detail
is unyielding.

PIETÀ

In the town where the hero was born you may:
gaze at the monument, admire its size,
shoo two chickens from the empty museum's steps,
ask for his mother's address,
knock, push the creaking door open.
Her bearing is erect, her hair is straight, her gaze is clear.
You may tell her that you've just arrived from Poland.
You may bear greetings. Make your questions loud and clear.
Yes, she loved him very much. Yes, he was born that way.
Yes, she was standing by the prison wall that morning.
Yes, she heard the shots.
You may regret not having brought a camera,
a tape recorder. Yes, she has seen such things.
She read his final letter on the radio.
She sang his favorite lullabies once on TV.
And once she even acted in a movie, in tears
from the bright lights. Yes, the memory still moves her.
Yes, just a little tired now. Yes, it will pass.
You may get up. Thank her. Say good-bye. Leave,
passing by the new arrivals in the hall.

INNOCENCE

Conceived on a mattress made of human hair.
Gerda. Erika. Maybe Margarete.
She doesn't know, no, not a thing about it.
This kind of knowledge isn't suited
to being passed on or absorbed.
The Greek Furies were too righteous.
Their birdy excess would rub us the wrong way.

Irma. Brigitte. Maybe Frederika.
She's twenty-two, perhaps a little older.
She knows the three languages that all travelers need.
The company she works for plans to export
the finest mattresses, synthetic fiber only.
Trade brings nations closer.

Berta. Ulrike. Maybe Hildegard.
Not beautiful perhaps, but tall and slim.
Cheeks, neck, breasts, thighs, belly
in full bloom now, shiny and new.
Blissfully barefoot on Europe's beaches,
she unbraids her bright hair, right down to her knees.

My advice: don't cut it (her hairdresser says)
once you have, it'll never grow back so thick.
Trust me.
It's been proved
tausend- und tausendmal.

VIETNAM

"Woman, what's your name?" "I don't know."
"How old are you? Where are you from?" "I don't know."
"Why did you dig that burrow?" "I don't know."
"How long have you been hiding?" "I don't know."
"Why did you bite my finger?" "I don't know."
"Don't you know that we won't hurt you?" "I don't know."
"Whose side are you on?" "I don't know."
"This is war, you've got to choose." "I don't know."
"Does your village still exist?" "I don't know."
"Are those your children?" "Yes."

WRITTEN IN A HOTEL

Kyoto is fortunate,
fortunate and full of palaces,
winged roofs,
stairs like musical scales.
Aged but flirtatious,
stony but alive,
wooden,
but growing from sky to earth,
Kyoto is a city
whose beauty moves you to tears.

I mean the real tears
of a certain gentleman,
a connoisseur, lover of antiquities,
who at a key moment
from behind a green table,
exclaimed that after all
there are so many inferior cities
and burst out sobbing
in his seat.

That's how Kyoto, far lovelier
than Hiroshima, was saved.

But this is ancient history.
I can't dwell on it forever
or keep asking endlessly,
what's next, what's next.

Day to day I trust in permanence,
in history's prospects.
How can I sink my teeth into apples
in a constant state of terror.

Now and then I hear about some Prometheus
wearing his fire helmet,
enjoying his grandkids.

While writing these lines
I wonder
what in them will come to sound
ridiculous and when.

Fear strikes me
only at times.
On the road.
In a strange city.

With garden-variety brick walls,
a tower, old and ordinary,
stucco peeling under slapdash moldings,
cracker-box housing projects,
nothing,
a helpless little tree.

What would he do here,
that tenderhearted gentleman,
the connoisseur, lover of antiquities.

Plaster god, have mercy on him.
Heave a sigh, oh classic,
from the depths of your mass-produced bust.

Only now and then,
in a city, one of many.
In a hotel room
overlooking the gutter
with a cat howling like a baby
under the stars.

In a city with lots of people,
many more than you'll find painted
on jugs, cups, saucers, and silk screens.

In a city about which I know
this one thing:
it's not Kyoto,
not Kyoto for sure.

A FILM FROM THE SIXTIES

This adult male. This person on earth.
Ten billion nerve cells. Ten pints of blood
pumped by ten ounces of heart.
This object took three billion years to emerge.

He first took the shape of a small boy.
The boy would lean his head on his aunt's knees.
Where is that boy. Where are those knees.
The little boy got big. Those were the days.
These mirrors are cruel and smooth as asphalt.
Yesterday he ran over a cat. Yes, not a bad idea.
The cat was saved from this age's hell.
A girl in a car checked him out.
No, her knees weren't what he's looking for.
Anyway he just wants to lie in the sand and breathe.
He has nothing in common with the world.
He feels like a handle broken off a jug,
but the jug doesn't know it's broken and keeps going to the well.
It's amazing. Someone's still willing to work.
The house gets built. The doorknob has been carved.
The tree is grafted. The circus will go on.
The whole won't go to pieces, although it's made of them.
Thick and heavy as glue *sunt lacrimae rerum*.
But all that's only background, incidental.
Within him, there's awful darkness, in the darkness a small boy.

God of humor, do something about him, OK?
God of humor, do something about him today.

REPORT FROM THE HOSPITAL

We used matches to draw lots: who would visit him.
And I lost. I got up from our table.
Visiting hours were just about to start.

When I said hello he didn't say a word.
I tried to take his hand—he pulled it back
like a hungry dog that won't give up his bone.

He seemed embarrassed about dying.
What do you say to someone like that?
Our eyes never met, like in a faked photograph.

He didn't care if I stayed or left.
He didn't ask about anyone from our table.
Not you, Barry. Or you, Larry. Or you, Harry.

My head started aching. Who's dying on whom?
I went on about modern medicine and the three violets in a jar.
I talked about the sun and faded out.

It's a good thing they have stairs to run down.
It's a good thing they have gates to let you out.
It's a good thing you're all waiting at our table.

The hospital smell makes me sick.

RETURNING BIRDS

This spring the birds came back again too early.
Rejoice, O reason: instinct can err, too.
It gathers wool, it dozes off—and down they fall
into the snow, into a foolish fate, a death
that doesn't suit their well-wrought throats and splendid claws,
their honest cartilage and conscientious webbing,
the heart's sensible sluice, the entrails' maze,
the nave of ribs, the vertebrae in stunning enfilades,
feathers deserving their own wing in any crafts museum,
the Benedictine patience of the beak.

This is not a dirge—no, it's only indignation.
An angel made of earthbound protein,
a living kite with glands straight from the Song of Songs,
singular in air, without number in the hand,
its tissues tied into a common knot
of place and time, as in an Aristotelian drama
unfolding to the wings' applause,
falls down and lies beside a stone,
which in its own archaic, simpleminded way
sees life as a chain of failed attempts.

THOMAS MANN

Dear mermaids, it was bound to happen.
Beloved fauns and honorable angels,
evolution has emphatically cast you out.
Not that it lacks imagination, but
you with your Devonian tail fins and alluvial breasts,
your fingered hands and cloven feet,
your arms alongside, not instead of, wings,
your, heaven help us, diphyletic skeletons,
your ill timed tails, horns sprouted out of spite,
illegitimate beaks, this morphogenetic potpourri, those
finned or furry frills and furbelows, the couplets
pairing human/heron with such cunning
that their offspring knows all, is immortal, and can fly,
you must admit that it would be a nasty joke,
excessive, everlasting, and no end of bother,
one that mother nature wouldn't like and won't allow.

And after all she does permit a fish to fly,
deft and defiant. Each such ascent
consoles our rule-bound world, reprieves it
from necessity's confines—more
than enough for the world to be a world.

And after all she does permit us baroque gems
like this: a platypus that feeds its chicks on milk.
She might have said no—and which of us would know
that we'd been robbed?

> But the best is that
she somehow missed the moment when a mammal turned up
with its hand miraculously feathered by a fountain pen.

TARSIER

I am a tarsier and a tarsier's son,
the grandson and great-grandson of tarsiers,
a tiny creature, made up of two pupils
and whatever simply could not be left out;
miraculously saved from further alterations—
since I'm no one's idea of a treat,
my coat's too small for a fur collar,
my glands provide no bliss,
and concerts go on without my gut—
I, a tarsier,
sit living on a human fingertip.

Good morning, lord and master,
what will you give me
for not taking anything from me?
How will you reward me for your own magnanimity?
What price will you set on my priceless head
for the poses I strike to make you smile?

My good lord is gracious,
my good lord is kind.
Who else could bear such witness if there were
no creatures unworthy of death?
You yourselves, perhaps?
But what you've come to know about yourselves
will serve for a sleepless night from star to star.

And only we few who remain unstripped of fur,
untorn from bone, unplucked of soaring feathers,
esteemed in all our quills, scales, tusks, and horns,
and in whatever else that ingenious protein
has seen fit to clothe us with,
we, my lord, are your dream,
which finds you innocent for now.

I am a tarsier—the father and grandfather of tarsiers—
a tiny creature, nearly half of something,
yet nonetheless a whole no less than others,
so light that twigs spring up beneath my weight
and might have lifted me to heaven long ago
if I hadn't had to fall
time and again
like a stone lifted from hearts
grown oh so sentimental:
I, a tarsier,
know well how essential it is to be a tarsier.

TO MY HEART, ON SUNDAY

Thank you, my heart:
you don't dawdle, you keep going
with no flattery or reward,
just from inborn diligence.

You get seventy credits a minute.
Each of your systoles
shoves a little boat
to open sea
to sail around the world.

Thank you, my heart:
time after time
you pluck me, separate even in sleep,
out of the whole.

You make sure I don't dream my dreams
up to that final flight,
no wings required.

Thank you, my heart:
I woke up again
and even though it's Sunday,
the day of rest,
the usual preholiday rush
continues underneath my ribs.

THE ACROBAT

From trapeze to
to trapeze, in the hush that
that follows the drum roll's sudden pause, through
through the startled air, more swiftly than
than his body's weight, which once again
again is late for its own fall.

Solo. Or even less than solo,
less, because he's crippled, missing
missing wings, missing them so much
that he can't miss the chance
to soar on shamefully unfeathered
naked vigilance alone.

Arduous ease,
watchful agility,
and calculated inspiration. Do you see
how he waits to pounce in flight; do you know
how he plots from head to toe
against his very being; do you know, do you see
how cunningly he weaves himself through his own former shape
and works to seize this swaying world
by stretching out the arms he has conceived—

beautiful beyond belief at this passing
at this very passing moment that's just passed.

A PALAEOLITHIC FERTILITY FETISH

The Great Mother has no face.
Why would the Great Mother need a face.
The face cannot stay faithful to the body,
the face disturbs the body, it is undivine,
it disturbs the body's solemn unity.
The Great Mother's visage is her bulging belly
with its blind navel in the middle.

The Great Mother has no feet.
What would the Great Mother do with feet.
Where is she going to go.
Why would she go into the world's details.
She has gone just as far as she wants
and keeps watch in the workshops under her taut skin.

So there's a world out there? Well and good.
It's bountiful? Even better.
The children have somewhere to go, to run around,
something to look up to? Wonderful.
So much that it's still there while they're sleeping,
almost ridiculously whole and real?
It keeps on existing when their backs are turned?
That's just too much—it shouldn't have.

The Great Mother barely has a pair of arms,
two tiny limbs lie lazing on her breasts.
Why would they want to bless life,
give gifts to what has enough and more!
Their only obligation is to endure as long as earth and sky
just in case
of some mishap that never comes.
To form a zigzag over essence.
The ornament's last laugh.

CAVE

There's nothing on the walls
except for dampness.
It's cold and dark in here.

But cold and dark
after a burnt-out fire.
Nothing, but nothing remaining
from a bison drawn in ocher.

Nothing—but a nothing left
after the long resistance
of the beast's lowered brow.
So, a Beautiful Nothing.
Deserving a capital letter.
A heresy against humdrum nothingness,
unconverted and proud of the difference.

Nothing—but after us,
who were here before
and ate our hearts
and drank our blood.

Nothing, to wit:
our unfinished dance.
Your first thighs, arms, necks, faces
by the fire.
My first sacred bellies
filled with minuscule Pascals.

Silence, but after voices.
Not a sluggish sort of silence.
A silence that had its own throats once,
its flutes and tambourines.
Grafted here like a wilding
by laughter and howls.

Silence—but in darkness
exalted by eyelids.
Darkness—but in cold
penetrating skin and bone.
Coldness—but of death.

On earth, maybe an earth
in a sky that might be seventh heaven?

Launched headfirst from the void,
you'd love to know.

MOTION

You're crying here, but there they're dancing,
there they're dancing in your tear.
There they're happy, making merry,
they don't know a blessed thing.
Almost the glimmering of mirrors.
Almost candles flickering.
Nearly staircases and hallways.
Gestures, lace cuffs, so it seems.
Hydrogen, oxygen, those rascals.
Chlorine, sodium, a pair of rogues.
The fop nitrogen parading
up and down, around, about
beneath the vault, inside the dome.
Your crying's music to their ears.
Yes, *eine kleine Nachtmusik*.
Who are you, lovely masquerader.

So he's got to have happiness,
he's got to have truth, too,
he's got to have eternity—
did you ever!

He has only just learned to tell dreams from waking;
only just realized that he is he;
only just whittled with his hand né fin
a flint, a rocket ship;
easily drowned in the ocean's teaspoon,
not even funny enough to tickle the void;
sees only with his eyes;
hears only with his ears;
his speech's personal best is the conditional;
he uses his reason to pick holes in reason.
In short, he's next to no one,
but his head's full of freedom, omniscience, and the Being
beyond his foolish meat—
did you ever!

For he does apparently exist.
He genuinely came to be
beneath one of the more parochial stars.
He's lively and quite active in his fashion.
His capacity for wonder is well advanced
for a crystal's deviant descendant.
And considering his difficult childhood
spent kowtowing to the herd's needs,
he's already quite an individual indeed—
did you ever!

Carry on, then, if only for the moment
that it takes a tiny galaxy to blink!
One wonders what will become of him,
since he does in fact seem to be.

And as far as being goes, he really tries quite hard.
Quite hard indeed—one must admit.
With that ring in his nose, with that toga, that sweater.
He's no end of fun, for all you say.
Poor little beggar.
A human, if ever we saw one.

COULD HAVE

It could have happened.
It had to happen.
It happened earlier. Later.
Nearer. Farther off.
It happened, but not to you.

You were saved because you were the first.
You were saved because you were the last.
Alone. With others.
On the right. The left.
Because it was raining. Because of the shade.
Because the day was sunny.

You were in luck—there was a forest.
You were in luck—there were no trees.
You were in luck—a rake, a hook, a beam, a brake,
a jamb, a turn, a quarter inch, an instant.
You were in luck   just then a straw went floating by.

As a result, because, although, despite.
What would have happened if a hand, a foot,
within an inch, a hairsbreadth from
an unfortunate coincidence.

So you're here? Still dizzy from another dodge, close shave,
     reprieve?
One hole in the net and you slipped through?
I couldn't be more shocked or speechless.
Listen,
how your heart pounds inside me.

FALLING FROM THE SKY

Magic is dying out, although the heights
still pulse with its vast force. On August nights
you can't be sure what's falling from the sky:
a star? or something else that still belongs on high?
Is making wishes an old-fashioned blunder
if heaven only knows what we are under?
Above our modern heads the dark's still dark,
but can't some twinkle in it explain: "I'm a spark,
I swear, a flash that a comet shook loose
from its tail, just a bit of cosmic rubble;
it's not me falling in tomorrow's news,
that's some other spark nearby, having engine trouble."

WRONG NUMBER

At midnight, in an empty, hushed art gallery
a tactless telephone spews forth a stream of rings;
a human sleeping now would jump up instantly,
but only sleepless prophets and untiring kings
reside here, where the moonlight makes them pale;
they hold their breath, their eyes fixed on some nail
or crack; only the young pawnbroker's bride
seems taken by that odd, ringing contraption,
but even she won't lay her fan aside,
she too just hangs there, caught in mid-nonaction.
Above it all, in scarlet robes or nude,
they view nocturnal fuss as simply rude.
Here's more black humor worthy of the name
than if some grand duke leaned out from his frame
and vented his frustration with a vulgar curse.
And if some silly man calling from town
refuses to give up, put the receiver down,
though he's got the wrong number? He lives, so he errs.

THEATRE IMPRESSIONS

For me the tragedy's most important act is the sixth:
the raising of the dead from the stage's battlegrounds,
the straightening of wigs and fancy gowns,
removing knives from stricken breasts,
taking nooses from lifeless necks,
lining up among the living
to face the audience.

The bows, both solo and ensemble—
the pale hand on the wounded heart,
the curtsies of the hapless suicide,
the bobbing of the chopped-off head.

The bows in pairs—
rage extends its arm to meekness,
the victim's eyes smile at the torturer,
the rebel indulgently walks beside the tyrant.

Eternity trampled by the golden slipper's toe.
Redeeming values swept aside with the swish of a
    wide-brimmed hat.
The unrepentant urge to start all over tomorrow.

Now enter, single file, the hosts who died early on,
in Acts 3 and 4, or between scenes.
The miraculous return of all those lost without a trace.

The thought that they've been waiting patiently offstage
without taking off their makeup
or their costumes
moves me more than all the tragedy's tirades.

But the curtain's fall is the most uplifting part,
the things you see before it hits the floor:
here one hand quickly reaches for a flower,

there another hand picks up a fallen sword.
Only then, one last, unseen, hand
does its duty
and grabs me by the throat.

VOICES

You can't move an inch, my dear Marcus Emilius,
without Aborigines sprouting up as if from the earth itself.

Your heel sticks fast amidst Rutulians.
You founder knee-deep in Sabines and Latins.
You're up to your waist, your neck, your nostrils
in Aequians and Volscians, dear Lucius Fabius.

These irksome little nations, thick as flies.
It's enough to make you sick, dear Quintus Decius.

One town, then the next, then the hundred and seventieth.
The Fidenates' stubbornness. The Feliscans' ill will.
The shortsighted Ecetrans. The capricious Antemnates.
The Labicanians and Pelignians, offensively aloof.
They drive us mild-mannered sorts to sterner measures
with every new mountain we cross, dear Gaius Cloelius.

If only they weren't always in the way, the Auruncians, the
    Marsians,
but they always do get in the way, dear Spurius Manlius.

Tarquinians where you'd least expect them, Etruscans on all sides.
If that weren't enough, Volsinians and Veientians.
The Aulertians, beyond all reason. And, of course,
the endlessly vexatious Sapinians, my dear Sextus Oppius.

Little nations do have little minds.
The circle of thick skulls expands around us.
Reprehensible customs. Backward laws.
Ineffectual gods, my dear Titus Vilius.

Heaps of Hernicians. Swarms of Murricinians.
Antlike multitudes of Vestians and Samnites.
The farther you go, the more there are, dear Servius Follius.

These little nations are pitiful indeed.
Their foolish ways require supervision
with every new river we ford, dear Aulus Iunius.

Every new horizon threatens me.
That's how I'd put it, my dear Hostius Melius.

To which I, Hostus Melius, would reply, my dear
Appius Papius: March on! The world has got to end somewhere.

THE LETTERS OF THE DEAD

We read the letters of the dead like helpless gods,
but gods, nonetheless, since we know the dates that follow.
We know which debts will never be repaid.
Which widows will remarry with the corpse still warm.
Poor dead, blindfolded dead,
gullible, fallible, pathetically prudent.
We see the faces people make behind their backs.
We catch the sound of wills being ripped to shreds.
The dead sit before us comically, as if on buttered bread,
or frantically pursue the hats blown from their heads.
Their bad taste, Napoleon, steam, electricity,
their fatal remedies for curable diseases,
their foolish apocalypse according to St. John,
their counterfeit heaven on earth according to Jean-Jacques. . . .
We watch the pawns on their chessboards in silence,
even though we see them three squares later.
Everything the dead predicted has turned out completely different.
Or a little bit different—which is to say, completely different.
The most fervent of them gaze confidingly into our eyes:
their calculations tell them that they'll find perfection there.

OLD FOLKS' HOME

Here comes Her Highness—well you know who I mean,
our Helen the snooty—now who made her queen!
With her lipstick and wig on, as if we could care,
like her three sons in heaven can see her from there!

"I wouldn't be here if they'd lived through the war.
I'd spend winter with one son, summer with another."
What makes her so sure?
I'd be dead too now, with her for a mother.

And she keeps on asking ("I don't mean to pry")
why from your sons and daughters there's never a word
even though they weren't killed. "If my boys were alive,
I'd spend all my holidays home with the third."

Right, and in his gold carriage he'd come and get her,
drawn by a swan or a lily-white dove,
to show all of us that he'll never forget her
and how much he owes to her motherly love.

Even Jane herself, the nurse, can't help but grin
when our Helen starts singing this old song again—
even though Jane's job is commiseration
Monday through Friday, with two weeks' vacation.

ADVERTISEMENT

I'm a tranquilizer.
I'm effective at home.
I work in the office.
I can take exams
or the witness stand.
I mend broken cups with care.
All you have to do is take me,
let me melt beneath your tongue,
just gulp me
with a glass of water.

I know how to handle misfortune,
how to take bad news.
I can minimize injustice,
lighten up God's absence,
or pick the widow's veil that suits your face.
What are you waiting for—
have faith in my chemical compassion.

You're still a young man/woman.
It's not too late to learn how to unwind.
Who said
you have to take it on the chin?

Let me have your abyss.
I'll cushion it with sleep.
You'll thank me for giving you
four paws to fall on.

Sell me your soul.
There are no other takers.

There is no other devil anymore.

LAZARUS TAKES A WALK

The professor has died three times now.
After the first death, he was taught to move his head.
After the second, he learned how to sit up.
After the third, they even got him on his feet,
propped up by a sturdy, chubby nanny:
Let's take a little walk, shall we, professor?

Severe brain damage following the accident
and yet—will wonders never cease—he's come so far:
left right, light dark, tree grass, hurt eat.

Two plus two, professor?
Two, says the professor.
At least he's getting warm.

Hurt, grass, sit, bench.
But at the garden's edge, that old bird,
neither pink nor cheery,
chased away three times now,
his real nanny. Or so she says—who knows.

He wants to go to her. Another tantrum.
What a shame. This time he came so close.

SNAPSHOT OF A CROWD

In the snapshot of a crowd,
my head's seventh from the edge,
or maybe fourth from the left,
or twenty-eighth from the bottom;

my head is I don't know which,
no longer on its own shoulders,
just like the rest (and vice versa),
neither clearly male nor female;

whatever it signifies
is of no significance,

and the Spirit of the Age
may just glance its way, at best;

my head is statistical,
it consumes its steel *per capita*
globally and with composure;

shamelessly predictable,
complacently replaceable;

as if I didn't even own it
in my own and separate way;

as if it were one skull of many
found unnamed in strip-mined graveyards
and preserved so well that one
forgets that its owner's gone;

as if it were already there,
my head, any-, everyone's—

where its memories, if any,
must reach deep into the future.

GOING HOME

He came home. Said nothing.
It was clear, though, that something had gone wrong.
He lay down fully dressed.
Pulled the blanket over his head.
Tucked up his knees.
He's nearly forty, but not at the moment.
He exists just as he did inside his mother's womb,
clad in seven walls of skin, in sheltered darkness.
Tomorrow he'll give a lecture
on homeostasis in megagalactic cosmonautics.
For now, though, he has curled up and gone to sleep.

DISCOVERY

I believe in the great discovery.
I believe in the man who will make the discovery.
I believe in the fear of the man who will make the discovery.

I believe in his face going white,
his queasiness, his upper lip drenched in cold sweat.

I believe in the burning of his notes,
burning them into ashes,
burning them to the last scrap.

I believe in the scattering of numbers,
scattering them without regret.

I believe in the man's haste,
in the precision of his movements,
in his free will.

I believe in the shattering of tablets,
the pouring out of liquids,
the extinguishing of rays.

I am convinced this will end well,
that it will not be too late,
that it will take place without witnesses.

I'm sure no one will find out what happened,
not the wife, not the wall,
not even the bird that might squeal in its song.

I believe in the refusal to take part.
I believe in the ruined career.
I believe in the wasted years of work.
I believe in the secret taken to the grave.

These words soar for me beyond all rules
without seeking support from actual examples.
My faith is strong, blind, and without foundation.

DINOSAUR SKELETON

Beloved Brethren,
we have before us an example of incorrect proportions.
Behold! the dinosaur's skeleton looms above—

Dear Friends,
on the left we see the tail trailing into one infinity,
on the right, the neck juts into another—

Esteemed Comrades,
in between, four legs that finally mired in the slime
beneath this hillock of a trunk—

Gentle Citizens,
nature does not err, but it loves its little joke:
please note the laughably small head—

Ladies, Gentlemen,
a head this size does not have room for foresight,
and that is why its owner is extinct—

Honored Dignitaries,
a mind too small, an appetite too large,
more senseless sleep than prudent apprehension—

Distinguished Guests,
we're in far better shape in this regard,
life is beautiful and the world is ours—

Venerated Delegation,
the starry sky above the thinking reed
and moral law within it—

Most Reverend Deputation,
such success does not come twice
and perhaps beneath this single sun alone—

Inestimable Council,
how deft the hands,
how eloquent the lips,
what a head on these shoulders—

Supremest of Courts,
so much responsibility in place of a vanished tail—

A SPEECH AT THE LOST-AND-FOUND

I lost a few goddesses while moving south to north,
and also some gods while moving east to west.
I let several stars go out for good, they can't be traced.
An island or two sank on me, they're lost at sea.
I'm not even sure exactly where I left my claws,
who's got my fur coat, who's living in my shell.
My siblings died the day I left for dry land
and only one small bone recalls that anniversary in me.
I've shed my skin, squandered vertebrae and legs,
taken leave of my senses time and again.
I've long since closed my third eye to all that,
washed my fins of it and shrugged my branches.

Gone, lost, scattered to the four winds. It still surprises me
how little now remains, one first person sing., temporarily
declined in human form, just now making such a fuss
about a blue umbrella left yesterday on a bus.

ASTONISHMENT

Why after all this one and not the rest?
Why this specific self, not in a nest,
but a house? Sewn up not in scales, but skin?
Not topped off by a leaf, but by a face?
Why on earth now, on Tuesday of all days,
and why on earth, pinned down by this star's pin?
In spite of years of my not being here?
In spite of seas of all these dates and fates,
these cells, celestials, and coelenterates?
What is it really that made me appear
neither an inch nor half a globe too far,
neither a minute nor aeons too early?
What made me fill myself with me so squarely?
Why am I staring now into the dark
and muttering this unending monologue
just like the growling thing we call a dog?

BIRTHDAY

So much world all at once—how it rustles and bustles!
Moraines and morays and morasses and mussels,
the flame, the flamingo, the flounder, the feather—
how to line them all up, how to put them together?
All the thickets and crickets and creepers and creeks!
The beeches and leeches alone could take weeks.
Chinchillas, gorillas, and sarsaparillas—
thanks so much, but all this excess of kindness could kill us.
Where's the jar for this burgeoning burdock, brooks' babble,
rooks' squabble, snakes' squiggle, abundance, and trouble?
How to plug up the gold mines and pin down the fox,
how to cope with the lynx, bobolinks, streptococs!
Take dioxide: a lightweight, but mighty in deeds;
what about octopodes, what about centipedes?
I could look into prices, but don't have the nerve:
these are products I just can't afford, don't deserve.
Isn't sunset a little too much for two eyes
that, who knows, may not open to see the sun rise?
I am just passing through, it's a five-minute stop.
I won't catch what is distant; what's too close, I'll mix up.
While trying to plumb what the void's inner sense is,
I'm bound to pass by all these poppies and pansies.
What a loss when you think how much effort was spent
perfecting this petal, this pistil, this scent
for the one-time appearance, which is all they're allowed,
so aloofly precise and so fragilely proud.

INTERVIEW WITH A CHILD

The Master hasn't been among us long.
That's why he lies in wait in every corner.
Covers his eyes and peeks through the cracks.
Faces the wall, then suddenly turns around.

The Master rejects outright the ridiculous thought
that a table out of sight goes on being a table nonstop,
that a chair behind our backs stays stuck in chairlike bounds
and doesn't even try to fly the coop.

True, it's hard to catch the world being different.
The apple tree slips back under the window before you can blink.
Incandescent sparrows always grow dim just in time.
Little pitchers have big ears and pick up every sound.
The nighttime closet acts as dull as its daytime twin.
The drawer does its best to assure the Master
it holds only what it's been given.
And no matter how fast you open the Brothers Grimm,
the princess always manages to take her seat again.

"They sense I'm a stranger here," the Master sighs,
"they won't let a new kid play their private games."

Since how can it be that whatever exists
can only exist in one way,
an awful situation, for there's no escaping yourself,
no pause, no transformation? In a humble from-here-to-here?
A fly caught in a fly? A mouse trapped in a mouse?
A dog never let off its latent chain?
A fire that can't come up with anything better
than burning the Master's trustful finger one more time?
Is this the definitive, actual world:
scattered wealth that can't be gathered,
useless luxury, forbidden options?

"No," the Master cries, and stomps all the feet
he can muster—for such great despair
that beetle's six legs wouldn't be enough.

ALLEGRO MA NON TROPPO

Life, you're beautiful (I say)
you just couldn't get more fecund,
more befrogged or nightingaley,
more anthillful or sproutspouting.

I'm trying to court life's favor,
to get into its good graces,
to anticipate its whims.
I'm always the first to bow,

always there where it can see me
with my humble, reverent face,
soaring on the wings of rapture,
falling under waves of wonder.

Oh how grassy is this hopper,
how this berry ripely rasps.
I would never have conceived it
if I weren't conceived myself!

Life (I say) I've no idea
what I could compare you to.
No one else can make a pine cone
and then make the pine cone's clone.

I praise your inventiveness,
bounty, sweep, exactitude,
sense of order—gifts that border
on witchcraft and wizardry.

I just don't want to upset you,
tease or anger, vex or rile.
For millennia, I've been trying
to appease you with my smile.

I tug at life by its leaf hem:
will it stop for me, just once,
momentarily forgetting
to what end it runs and runs?

AUTOTOMY

In danger, the holothurian cuts itself in two.
It abandons one self to a hungry world
and with the other self it flees.

It violently divides into doom and salvation,
retribution and reward, what has been and what will be.

An abyss appears in the middle of its body
between what instantly become two foreign shores.

Life on one shore, death on the other.
Here hope and there despair.

If there are scales, the pans don't move.
If there is justice, this is it.

To die just as required, without excess.
To grow back just what's needed from what's left.

We, too, can divide ourselves, it's true.
But only into flesh and a broken whisper.
Into flesh and poetry.

The throat on one side, laughter on the other,
quiet, quickly dying out.

Here the heavy heart, there *non omnis moriar*—
just three little words, like a flight's three feathers.

The abyss doesn't divide us.
The abyss surrounds us.

In memoriam Halina Poświatowska

FROZEN MOTION

This isn't Miss Duncan, the noted danseuse?
Not the drifting cloud, the wafting zephyr, the Bacchante,
moonlit waters, waves swaying, breezes sighing?

Standing this way, in the photographer's atelier,
heftily, fleshily wrested from music and motion,
she's cast to the mercies of a pose,
forced to bear false witness.

Thick arms raised above her head,
a knotted knee protrudes from her short tunic,
left leg forward, naked foot and toes,
with 5 (count them) toenails.

One short step from eternal art into artificial eternity—
I reluctantly admit that it's better than nothing
and more fitting than otherwise.

Behind the screen, a pink corset, a handbag,
in it a ticket for a steamship
leaving tomorrow, that is, sixty years ago;
never again, but still at nine a.m. sharp.

CERTAINTY

"Thou art certain,* then, our ship hath touch'd upon
the deserts of Bohemia?" "Aye, my lord." The quote's
from Shakespeare, who, I'm certain, wasn't someone else.
Some facts and dates, a portrait nearly done before
his death . . . Who needs more? Why expect to see
the proof, snatched up once by the Greater Sea,
then cast upon this world's Bohemian shore?

---

*Changed from Shakespeare's "perfect." *[Translators' note]*

THE CLASSIC

A few clods of dirt, and his life will be forgotten.
The music will break free from circumstance.
No more coughing of the maestro over minuets.
Poultices will be torn off.
Fire will consume the dusty, lice-ridden wig.
Ink spots will vanish from the lace cuff.
The shoes, inconvenient witnesses, will be tossed on the trash heap.
The least gifted of his pupils will get the violin.
Butchers' bills will be removed from between the music sheets.
His poor mother's letters will line the stomachs of mice.
The ill-fated love will fade away.
Eyes will stop shedding tears.
The neighbors' daughter will find a use for the pink ribbon.
The age, thank God, isn't Romantic yet.
Everything that's not a quartet
will become a forgettable fifth.
Everything that's not a quintet
will become a superfluous sixth.
Everything that's not a choir made of forty angels
will fall silent, reduced to barking dogs, a gendarme's belch.
The aloe plant will be taken from the window
along with a dish of fly poison and the pomade pot,
and the view of the garden (oh yes!) will be revealed—
the garden that was never here.
Now hark! ye mortals, listen, listen now,
take heed, in rapt amazement,
o rapt, o stunned, o heedful mortals, listen,
o listeners—now listen—be all ears—

IN PRAISE OF DREAMS

In my dreams
I paint like Vermeer van Delft.

I speak fluent Greek
and not just with the living.

I drive a car
that does what I want it to.

I am gifted
and write mighty epics.

I hear voices
as clearly as any venerable saint.

My brilliance as a pianist
would stun you.

I fly the way we ought to,
i.e., on my own.

Falling from the roof,
I tumble gently to the grass.

I've got no problem
breathing under water.

I can't complain:
I've been able to locate Atlantis.

It's gratifying that I can always
wake up before dying.

As soon as war breaks out,
I roll over on my other side.

I'm a child of my age,
but I don't have to be.

A few years ago
I saw two suns.

And the night before last a penguin,
clear as day.

TRUE LOVE

True love. Is it normal,
is it serious, is it practical?
What does the world get from two people
who exist in a world of their own?

Placed on the same pedestal for no good reason,
drawn randomly from millions, but convinced
it had to happen this way—in reward for what? For nothing.
The light descends from nowhere.
Why on these two and not on others?
Doesn't this outrage justice? Yes it does.
Doesn't it disrupt our painstakingly erected principles,
and cast the moral from the peak? Yes on both accounts.

Look at the happy couple.
Couldn't they at least try to hide it,
fake a little depression for their friends' sake!
Listen to them laughing—it's an insult.
The language they use—deceptively clear.
And their little celebrations, rituals,
the elaborate mutual routines—
it's obviously a plot behind the human race's back!

It's hard even to guess how far things might go
if people start to follow their example.
What could religion and poetry count on?
What would be remembered? what renounced?
Who'd want to stay within bounds?

True love. Is it really necessary?
Tact and common sense tell us to pass over it in silence,
like a scandal in Life's highest circles.
Perfectly good children are born without its help.
It couldn't populate the planet in a million years,
it comes along so rarely.

Let the people who never find true love
keep saying that there's no such thing.

Their faith will make it easier for them to live and die.

My apologies to chance for calling it necessity.
My apologies to necessity if I'm mistaken, after all.
Please, don't be angry, happiness, that I take you as my due.
May my dead be patient with the way my memories fade.
My apologies to time for all the world I overlook each second.
My apologies to past loves for thinking that the latest is the first.
Forgive me, distant wars, for bringing flowers home.
Forgive me, open wounds, for pricking my finger.
I apologize for my record of minuets to those who cry from
    the depths.
I apologize to those who wait in railway stations for being asleep
    today at five a.m.
Pardon me, hounded hope, for laughing from time to time.
Pardon me, deserts, that I don't rush to you bearing a spoonful
    of water.
And you, falcon, unchanging year after year, always in the
    same cage,
your gaze always fixed on the same point in space,
forgive me, even if it turns out you were stuffed.
My apologies to the felled tree for the table's four legs.
My apologies to great questions for small answers.
Truth, please don't pay me much attention.
Dignity, please be magnanimous.
Bear with me, O mystery of existence, as I pluck the occasional
    thread from your train.
Soul, don't take offense that I've only got you now and then.
My apologies to everything that I can't be everywhere at once.
My apologies to everyone that I can't be each woman and
    each man.
I know I won't be justified as long as I live,
since I myself stand in my own way.
Don't bear me ill will, speech, that I borrow weighty words,
then labor heavily so that they may seem light.

A LARGE NUMBER

Four billion people on this earth,
but my imagination is still the same.
It's bad with large numbers.
It's still taken by particularity.
It flits in the dark like a flashlight,
illuminating only random faces
while all the rest go blindly by,
never coming to mind and never really missed.
But even a Dante couldn't get it right.
Let alone someone who is not.
Even with all the muses behind me.

Non omnis moriar—a premature worry.
But am I entirely alive and is that enough.
It never was, and now less than ever.
My choices are rejections, since there is no other way,
but what I reject is more numerous,
denser, more demanding than before.
A little poem, a sigh, at the cost of indescribable losses.
I whisper my reply to my stentorian calling.
I can't tell you how much I pass over in silence.
A mouse at the foot of the maternal mountain.
Life lasts as long as a few signs scratched by a claw in the sand.

My dreams—even they're not as populous as they should be.
They hold more solitude than noisy crowds.
Sometimes a long-dead friend stops by awhile.
A single hand turns the knob.

An echo's annexes overgrow the empty house.
I run from the doorstep into a valley
that is quiet, as if no one owned it, already an anachronism.

Why there's still all this space inside me
I don't know.

THANK-YOU NOTE

I owe so much
to those I don't love.

The relief as I agree
that someone else needs them more.

The happiness that I'm not
the wolf to their sheep.

The peace I feel with them,
the freedom—
love can neither give
nor take that.

I don't wait for them,
as in window-to-door-and-back.
Almost as patient
as a sundial,
I understand
what love can't,
and forgive
as love never would.

From a rendezvous to a letter
is just a few days or weeks,
not an eternity.

Trips with them always go smoothly,
concerts are heard,
cathedrals visited,
scenery is seen.

And when seven hills and rivers
come between us,
the hills and rivers
can be found on any map.

They deserve the credit
if I live in three dimensions,
in nonlyrical and nonrhetorical space
with a genuine, shifting horizon.

They themselves don't realize
how much they hold in their empty hands.

"I don't owe them a thing,"
would be love's answer
to this open question.

PSALM

Oh, the leaky boundaries of man-made states!
How many clouds float past them with impunity;
how much desert sand shifts from one land to another;
how many mountain pebbles tumble onto foreign soil
in provocative hops!

Need I mention every single bird that flies in the face of frontiers
or alights on the roadblock at the border?
A humble robin—still, its tail resides abroad
while its beak stays home. If that weren't enough, it won't stop
   bobbing!

Among innumerable insects, I'll single out only the ant
between the border guard's left and right boots
blithely ignoring the questions "Where from?" and "Where to?"

Oh, to register in detail, at a glance, the chaos
prevailing on every continent!
Isn't that a privet on the far bank
smuggling its hundred-thousandth leaf across the river?
And who but the octopus, with impudent long arms,
would disrupt the sacred bounds of territorial waters?

And how can we talk of order overall
when the very placement of the stars
leaves us doubting just what shines for whom?

Not to speak of the fog's reprehensible drifting!
And dust blowing all over the steppes
as if they hadn't been partitioned!
And the voices coasting on obliging airwaves,
that conspiratorial squeaking, those indecipherable mutters!

Only what is human can truly be foreign.
The rest is mixed vegetation, subversive moles, and wind.

LOT'S WIFE

They say I looked back out of curiosity.
But I could have had other reasons.
I looked back mourning my silver bowl.
Carelessly, while tying my sandal strap.
So I wouldn't have to keep staring at the righteous nape
of my husband Lot's neck.
From the sudden conviction that if I dropped dead
he wouldn't so much as hesitate.
From the disobedience of the meek.
Checking for pursuers.
Struck by the silence, hoping God had changed his mind.
Our two daughters were already vanishing over the hilltop.
I felt age within me. Distance.
The futility of wandering. Torpor.
I looked back setting my bundle down.
I looked back not knowing where to set my foot.
Serpents appeared on my path,
spiders, field mice, baby vultures.
They were neither good nor evil now—every living thing
was simply creeping or hopping along in the mass panic.
I looked back in desolation.
In shame because we had stolen away.
Wanting to cry out, to go home.
Or only when a sudden gust of wind
unbound my hair and lifted up my robe.
It seemed to me that they were watching from the walls of Sodom
and bursting into thunderous laughter again and again.
I looked back in anger.
To savor their terrible fate.
I looked back for all the reasons given above.
I looked back involuntarily.
It was only a rock that turned underfoot, growling at me.

It was a sudden crack that stopped me in my tracks.
A hamster on its hind paws tottered on the edge.
It was then we both glanced back.
No, no. I ran on,
I crept, I flew upward
until darkness fell from the heavens
and with it scorching gravel and dead birds.
I couldn't breathe and spun around and around.
Anyone who saw me must have thought I was dancing.
It's not inconceivable that my eyes were open.
It's possible I fell facing the city.

SEEN FROM ABOVE

A dead beetle lies on the path through the field.
Three pairs of legs folded neatly on its belly.
Instead of death's confusion, tidiness and order.
The horror of this sight is moderate,
its scope is strictly local, from the wheat grass to the mint.
The grief is quarantined.
The sky is blue.

To preserve our peace of mind, animals die
more shallowly: they aren't deceased, they're dead.
They leave behind, we'd like to think, less feeling and less world,
departing, we suppose, from a stage less tragic.
Their meek souls never haunt us in the dark,
they know their place,
they show respect.

And so the dead beetle on the path
lies unmourned and shining in the sun.
One glance at it will do for meditation—
clearly nothing much has happened to it.
Important matters are reserved for us,
for our life and our death, a death
that always claims the right of way.

EXPERIMENT

As a short subject before the main feature—
in which the actors did their best
to make me cry and even laugh—
we were shown an interesting experiment
involving a head.

The head
a minute earlier was still attached to . . .
but now it was cut off.
Everyone could see that it didn't have a body.
The tubes dangling from the neck hooked it up to a machine
that kept its blood circulating.
The head
was doing just fine.

Without showing pain or even surprise,
it followed a moving flashlight with its eyes.
It pricked up its ears at the sound of a bell.
Its moist nose could tell
the smell of bacon from odorless oblivion,
and licking its chops with evident relish
it salivated its salute to physiology.

A dog's faithful head,
a dog's friendly head
squinted its eyes when stroked,
convinced that it was still part of a whole
that crooks its back if patted
and wags its tail.

I thought about happiness and was frightened.
For if that's all life is about,
the head
was happy.

SMILES

The world would rather *see* hope than just hear
its song. And that's why statesmen have to smile.
Their pearly whites mean they're still full of cheer.
The game's complex, the goal's far out of reach,
the outcome's still unclear—once in a while,
we need a friendly, gleaming set of teeth.

Heads of state must display unfurrowed brows
on airport runways, in the conference room.
They must embody one big, toothy "Wow!"
while pressing flesh or pressing urgent issues.
Their faces' self-regenerating tissues
make our hearts hum and our lenses zoom.

Dentistry turned to diplomatic skill
promises us a Golden Age tomorrow.
The going's rough, and so we need the laugh
of bright incisors, molars of goodwill.
Our times are still not safe and sane enough
for faces to show ordinary sorrow.

Dreamers keep saying, "Human brotherhood
will make this place a smiling paradise."
I'm not convinced. The statesman, in that case,
would not require facial exercise,
except from time to time: he's feeling good,
he's glad it's spring, and so he moves his face.
But human beings are, by nature, sad.
So be it, then. It isn't all that bad.

THE TERRORIST, HE'S WATCHING

The bomb in the bar will explode at thirteen twenty.
Now it's just thirteen sixteen.
There's still time for some to go in,
and some to come out.

The terrorist has already crossed the street.
The distance keeps him out of danger,
and what a view—just like the movies:

A woman in a yellow jacket, she's going in.
A man in dark glasses, he's coming out.
Teenagers in jeans, they're talking.
Thirteen seventeen and four seconds.
The short one, he's lucky, he's getting on a scooter,
but the tall one, he's going in.

Thirteen seventeen and forty seconds.
That girl, she's walking along with a green ribbon in her hair.
But then a bus suddenly pulls in front of her.
Thirteen eighteen.
The girl's gone.
Was she that dumb, did she go in or not,
we'll see when they carry them out.

Thirteen nineteen.
Somehow no one's going in.
Another guy, fat, bald, is leaving, though.
Wait a second, looks like he's looking for something in his
   pockets and
at thirteen twenty minus ten seconds
he goes back in for his crummy gloves.

Thirteen twenty exactly.
This waiting, it's taking forever.

Any second now.
No, not yet.
Yes, now.
The bomb, it explodes.

A MEDIEVAL MINIATURE

Up the verdantest of hills,
in this most equestrian of pageants,
wearing the silkiest of cloaks.

Toward a castle with seven towers,
each of them by far the tallest.

In the foreground, a duke,
most flatteringly unrotund;
by his side, his duchess
young and fair beyond compare.

Behind them, the ladies-in-waiting,
all pretty as pictures, verily,
then a page, the most ladsome of lads,
and perched upon his pagey shoulder
something exceedingly monkeylike,
endowed with the drollest of faces
and tails.

Following close behind, three knights,
all chivalry and rivalry,
so if the first is fearsome of countenance,
the next one strives to be more daunting still,
and if he prances on a bay steed
the third will prance upon a bayer,
and all twelve hooves dance glancingly
atop the most wayside of daisies.

Whereas whosoever is downcast and weary,
cross-eyed and out at elbows,
is most manifestly left out of the scene.

Even the least pressing of questions,
burgherish or peasantish,
cannot survive beneath this most azure of skies.

And not even the eaglest of eyes
could spy even the tiniest of gallows—
nothing casts the slightest shadow of a doubt.

Thus they proceed most pleasantly
through this feudalest of realisms.

This same, however, has seen to the scene's balance:
it has given them their Hell in the next frame.
Oh yes, all that went without
even the silentest of sayings.

"Today he sings this way: tralala tra la.
But I sang it like this: tralala tra la.
Do you hear the difference?
And instead of standing here, he stands here
and looks this way, not this way,
although she comes flying in from over there,
not over there, and not like today rampa pampa pam,
but quite simply rampa pampa pam,
the unforgettable Tschubek-Bombonieri,
only
who remembers her now—"

IN PRAISE OF MY SISTER

My sister doesn't write poems,
and it's unlikely that she'll suddenly start writing poems.
She takes after her mother, who didn't write poems,
and also her father, who likewise didn't write poems.
I feel safe beneath my sister's roof:
my sister's husband would rather die than write poems.
And, even though this is starting to sound as repetitive as Peter
    Piper,
the truth is, none of my relatives write poems.

My sister's desk drawers don't hold old poems,
and her handbag doesn't hold new ones.
When my sister asks me over for lunch,
I know she doesn't want to read me her poems.
Her soups are delicious without ulterior motives.
Her coffee doesn't spill on manuscripts.

There are many families in which nobody writes poems,
but once it starts up it's hard to quarantine.
Sometimes poetry cascades down through the generations,
creating fatal whirlpools where family love may founder.

My sister has tackled oral prose with some success,
but her entire written opus consists of postcards from vacations
whose text is only the same promise every year:
when she gets back, she'll have
so much
much
much to tell.

HERMITAGE

You expected a hermit to live in the wilderness,
but he has a little house and a garden,
surrounded by cheerful birch groves,
ten minutes off the highway.
Just follow the signs.

You don't have to gaze at him through binoculars from afar.
You can see and hear him right up close,
while he's patiently explaining to a tour group from Wieliczka
why he's chosen strict isolation.

He wears a grayish habit,
and he has a long white beard,
cheeks pink as a baby's,
and bright-blue eyes.
He'll gladly pose before the rosebush
for color photographs.

His picture is being taken by one Stanley Kowalik of Chicago
who promises prints once they're developed.

Meanwhile a tight-lipped old lady from Bydgoszcz
whom no one visits but the meter reader
is writing in the guestbook:
"God be praised
for letting me
see a genuine hermit before I die."

Teenagers write, too, using knives on trees:
"The Spirituals of '75—meeting down below."

But what's Spot up to, where has Spot gone?
He's underneath the bench pretending he's a wolf.

PORTRAIT OF A WOMAN

She must be a variety.
Change so that nothing will change.
It's easy, impossible, tough going, worth a shot.
Her eyes are, as required, deep blue, gray,
dark, merry, full of pointless tears.
She sleeps with him as if she's first in line or the only one on
    earth.
She'll bear him four children, no children, one.
Naïve, but gives the best advice.
Weak, but takes on anything.
A screw loose and tough as nails.
Curls up with Jaspers or *Ladies' Home Journal.*
Can't figure out this bolt and builds a bridge.
Young, young as ever, still looking young.
Holds in her hands a baby sparrow with a broken wing,
her own money for some trip far away,
a meat cleaver, a compress, a glass of vodka.
Where's she running, isn't she exhausted.
Not a bit, a little, to death, it doesn't matter.
She must love him, or she's just plain stubborn.
For better, for worse, for heaven's sake.

EVALUATION OF AN UNWRITTEN POEM

In the poem's opening words
the authoress asserts that while the Earth is small,
the sky is excessively large and
in it there are, I quote, "too many stars for our own good."

In her depiction of the sky, one detects a certain helplessness,
the authoress is lost in a terrifying expanse,
she is startled by the planets' lifelessness,
and within her mind (which can only be called imprecise)
a question soon arises:
whether we are, in the end, alone
under the sun, all suns that ever shone.

In spite of all the laws of probability!
And today's universally accepted assumptions!
In the face of the irrefutable evidence that may fall
into human hands any day now! That's poetry for you.

Meanwhile, our Lady Bard returns to Earth,
a planet, so she claims, which "makes its rounds without
    eyewitnesses,"
the only "science fiction that our cosmos can afford."
The despair of a Pascal (1623–1662, *note mine*)
is, the authoress implies, unrivaled
on any, say, Andromeda or Cassiopeia.
Our solitary existence exacerbates our sense of obligation,
and raises the inevitable question, How are we to live et cetera?
since "we can't avoid the void."
" 'My God,' man calls out to Himself,
'have mercy on me, I beseech thee, show me the way . . .' "

The authoress is distressed by the thought of life squandered
    so freely,
as if our supplies were boundless.

She is likewise worried by wars, which are, in her perverse
    opinion,
always lost on both sides,
and by the "authoritorture" (*sic!*) of some people by others.
Her moralistic intentions glimmer throughout the poem.
They might shine brighter beneath a less naïve pen.

Not under this one, alas. Her fundamentally unpersuasive thesis
(that we may well be, in the end, alone
under the sun, all suns that ever shone)
combined with her lackadaisical style (a mixture
of lofty rhetoric and ordinary speech)
forces the question: Whom might this piece convince?
The answer can only be: No one. *Q.E.D.*

WARNING

Don't take jesters into outer space,
that's my advice.

Fourteen lifeless planets,
a few comets, two stars.
By the time you take off for the third star,
your jesters will be out of humor.

The cosmos is what it is—
namely, perfect.
Your jesters will never forgive it.

Nothing will make them happy:
not time (too immemorial),
not beauty (no flaws),
not gravity (no use for levity).
While others drop their jaws in awe,
the jesters will just yawn.

En route to the fourth star
things will only get worse.
Curdled smiles,
disrupted sleep and equilibrium,
idle chatter:
Remember that crow with the cheese in its beak,
the fly droppings on His Majesty's portrait,
the monkey in the steaming bath—
now that was living.

Narrow-minded.
They'll take Thursday over infinity any day.
Primitive.
Out of tune suits them better than the music of the spheres.
They're happiest in the cracks
between theory and practice,

cause and effect.
But this is Space, not Earth: everything's a perfect fit.

On the thirtieth planet
(with an eye to its impeccable desolation)
they'll refuse even to leave their cubicles:
"My head aches," they'll complain. "I stubbed my toe."

What a waste. What a disgrace.
So much good money lost in outer space.

THE ONION

The onion, now that's something else.
Its innards don't exist.
Nothing but pure onionhood
fills this devout onionist.
Oniony on the inside,
onionesque it appears.
It follows its own daimonion
without our human tears.

Our skin is just a cover-up
for the land where none dare go,
an internal inferno,
the anathema of anatomy.
In an onion there's only onion
from its top to its toe,
onionymous monomania,
unanimous omninudity.

At peace, of a piece,
internally at rest.
Inside it, there's a smaller one
of undiminished worth.
The second holds a third one,
the third contains a fourth.
A centripetal fugue.
Polyphony compressed.

Nature's rotundest tummy,
its greatest success story,
the onion drapes itself in its
own aureoles of glory.
We hold veins, nerves, and fat,
secretions' secret sections.
Not for us such idiotic
onionoid perfections.

THE SUICIDE'S ROOM

I'll bet you think the room was empty.
Wrong. There were three chairs with sturdy backs.
A lamp, good for fighting the dark.
A desk, and on the desk a wallet, some newspapers.
A carefree Buddha and a worried Christ.
Seven lucky elephants, a notebook in a drawer.
You think our addresses weren't in it?

No books, no pictures, no records, you guess?
Wrong. A comforting trumpet poised in black hands.
Saskia and her cordial little flower.
Joy the spark of gods.
Odysseus stretched on the shelf in life-giving sleep
after the labors of Book Five.
The moralists
with the golden syllables of their names
inscribed on finely tanned spines.
Next to them, the politicians braced their backs.

No way out? But what about the door?
No prospects? The window had other views.
His glasses
lay on the windowsill.
And one fly buzzed—that is, was still alive.

You think at least the note must tell us something.
But what if I say there was no note—
and he had so many friends, but all of us fit neatly
inside the empty envelope propped up against a cup.

IN PRAISE OF FEELING BAD ABOUT YOURSELF

The buzzard never says it is to blame.
The panther wouldn't know what scruples mean.
When the piranha strikes, it feels no shame.
If snakes had hands, they'd claim their hands were clean.

A jackal doesn't understand remorse.
Lions and lice don't waver in their course.
Why should they, when they know they're right?

Though hearts of killer whales may weigh a ton,
in every other way they're light.

On this third planet of the sun
among the signs of bestiality
a clear conscience is Number One.

LIFE WHILE-YOU-WAIT

Life While-You-Wait.
Performance without rehearsal.
Body without alterations.
Head without premeditation.

I know nothing of the role I play.
I only know it's mine, I can't exchange it.

I have to guess on the spot
just what this play's all about.

Ill-prepared for the privilege of living,
I can barely keep up with the pace that the action demands.
I improvise, although I loathe improvisation.
I trip at every step over my own ignorance.
I can't conceal my hayseed manners.
My instincts are for hammy histrionics.
Stage fright makes excuses for me, which humiliate me more.
Extenuating circumstances strike me as cruel.

Words and impulses you can't take back,
stars you'll never get counted,
your character like a raincoat you button on the run—
the pitiful results of all this unexpectedness.

If I could just rehearse one Wednesday in advance,
or repeat a single Thursday that has passed!
But here comes Friday with a script I haven't seen.
Is it fair, I ask
(my voice a little hoarse,
since I couldn't even clear my throat offstage).

You'd be wrong to think that it's just a slapdash quiz
taken in makeshift accommodations. Oh no.
I'm standing on the set and I see how strong it is.

The props are surprisingly precise.
The machine rotating the stage has been around even longer.
The farthest galaxies have been turned on.
Oh no, there's no question, this must be the premiere.
And whatever I do
will become forever what I've done.

ON THE BANKS OF THE STYX

Dear individual soul, this is the Styx.
The Styx, that's right. Why are you so perplexed?
As soon as Charon reads the prepared text
over the speakers, let the nymphs affix
your name badge and transport you to the banks.
(The nymphs? They fled your woods and joined the ranks
of personnel here.) Floodlights will reveal
piers built of reinforced concrete and steel,
and hovercrafts whose beelike buzz resounds
where Charon used to ply his wooden oar.
Mankind has multiplied, has burst its bounds:
nothing, sweet soul, is as it was before.
Skyscrapers, solid waste, and dirty air:
the scenery's been harmed beyond repair.
Safe and efficient transportation (millions
of souls served here, all races, creeds, and sexes)
requires urban planning: hence pavilions,
warehouses, dry docks, and office complexes.
Among the gods it's Hermes, my dear soul,
who makes all prophecies and estimations
when revolutions and wars take their toll—
our boats, of course, require reservations.
A one-way trip across the Styx is free:
the meters saying, "No Canadian dimes,
no tokens" are left standing, as you see,
but only to remind us of old times.
From Section Thau Four of the Alpha Pier
you're boarding hovercraft Sigma Sixteen—
it's packed with sweating souls, but in the rear
you'll find a seat (I've got it on my screen).
Now Tartarus (let me pull up the file)
is overbooked, too—no way we could stretch it.

Cramped, crumpled souls all dying to get out,
one last half drop of Lethe in my phial . . .
Not faith in the beyond, but only doubt
can make you, sorry soul, a bit less wretched.

UTOPIA

Island where all becomes clear.

Solid ground beneath your feet.

The only roads are those that offer access.

Bushes bend beneath the weight of proofs.

The Tree of Valid Supposition grows here
with branches disentangled since time immemorial.

The Tree of Understanding, dazzlingly straight and simple,
sprouts by the spring called Now I Get It.

The thicker the woods, the vaster the vista:
the Valley of Obviously.

If any doubts arise, the wind dispels them instantly.

Echoes stir unsummoned
and eagerly explain all the secrets of the worlds.

On the right a cave where Meaning lies.

On the left the Lake of Deep Conviction.
Truth breaks from the bottom and bobs to the surface.

Unshakable Confidence towers over the valley.
Its peak offers an excellent view of the Essence of Things.

For all its charms, the island is uninhabited,
and the faint footprints scattered on its beaches
turn without exception to the sea.

As if all you can do here is leave
and plunge, never to return, into the depths.

Into unfathomable life.

The admirable number pi:
three point one four one.
All the following digits are also initial,
five nine two because it never ends.
It can't be comprehended *six five three five* at a glance,
eight nine by calculation,
seven nine or imagination,
not even *three two three eight* by wit, that is, by comparison
four six to anything else
two six four three in the world.
The longest snake on earth calls it quits at about forty feet.
Likewise, snakes of myth and legend, though they may hold out a
    bit longer.
The pageant of digits comprising the number pi
doesn't stop at the page's edge.
It goes on across the table, through the air,
over a wall, a leaf, a bird's nest, clouds, straight into the sky,
through all the bottomless, bloated heavens.
Oh how brief—a mouse tail, a pigtail—is the tail of a comet!
How feeble the star's ray, bent by bumping up against space!
While here we have *two three fifteen three hundred nineteen*
my phone number your shirt size the year
nineteen hundred and seventy-three the sixth floor
the number of inhabitants sixty-five cents
hip measurement two fingers a charade, a code,
in which we find *hail to thee, blithe spirit, bird thou never wert*
alongside *ladies and gentlemen, no cause for alarm,*
as well as *heaven and earth shall pass away,*
but not the number pi, oh no, nothing doing,

it keeps right on with its rather remarkable *five,*
its uncommonly fine *eight,*
its far from final *seven,*
nudging, always nudging a sluggish eternity
to continue.

THE PEOPLE ON THE BRIDGE

1986

STAGE FRIGHT

Poets and writers.
So the saying goes.
That is poets aren't writers, but who—

Poets are poetry, writers are prose—

Prose can hold anything including poetry,
but in poetry there's only room for poetry—

In keeping with the poster that announces it
with a fin-de-siècle flourish of its giant P
framed in a winged lyre's strings
I shouldn't simply walk in, I should fly—

And wouldn't I be better off barefoot
to escape the clump and squeak
of cut-rate sneakers,
a clumsy ersatz angel—

If at least the dress were longer and more flowing
and the poems appeared not from a handbag but by sleight of hand,
dressed in their Sunday best from head to toe,
with bells on, ding to dong,
ab ab ba—

On the platform lurks a little table
suggesting séances, with gilded legs,
and on the little table smokes a little candlestick—

Which means
I've got to read by candlelight
what I wrote by the light of an ordinary bulb
to the typewriter's tap tap tap—

Without worrying in advance
if it was poetry
and if so, what kind—

The kind in which prose is inappropriate
or the kind which is apropos in prose—

And what's the difference,
seen now only in half-light
against a crimson curtain's
purple fringe?

SURPLUS

A new star has been discovered,
which doesn't mean that things have gotten brighter
or that something we've been missing has appeared.

The star is large and distant,
so distant that it's small,
even smaller than others
much smaller than it.
Small wonder, then, if we were struck with wonder;
as we would be if only we had the time.

The star's age, mass, location—
all this perhaps will do
for one doctoral dissertation
and a wine-and-cheese reception
in circles close to the sky:
the astronomer, his wife, friends, and relations,
casual, congenial, come as you are,
mostly chat on earthbound topics,
surrounded by cozy earthtones.

The star's superb,
but that's no reason
why we can't drink to the ladies
who are incalculably closer.

The star's inconsequential.
It has no impact on the weather, fashion, final score,
government shake-ups, moral crises, take-home pay.

No effect on propaganda or on heavy industry.
It's not reflected in a conference table's shine.
It's supernumerary in the light of life's numbered days.

What's the use of asking
under how many stars man is born
and under how many in a moment he will die.

A new one.
"At least show me where it is."
"Between that gray cloud's jagged edge
and the acacia twig over there on the left."
"I see," I say.

ARCHEOLOGY

Well, my poor man,
seems we've made some progress in my field.
Millennia have passed
since you first called me archeology.

I no longer require
your stone gods,
your ruins with legible inscriptions.

Show me your whatever
and I'll tell you who you were.
Something's bottom,
something's top.
A scrap of engine. A picture tube's neck.
An inch of cable. Fingers turned to dust.
Or even less than that, or even less.

Using a method
that you couldn't have known then,
I can stir up memory
in countless elements.
Traces of blood are forever.
Lies shine.
Secret codes resound.
Doubts and intentions come to light.

If I want to
(and you can't be too sure
that I will),
I'll peer down the throat of your silence,
I'll read your views
from the sockets of your eyes,
I'll remind you in infinite detail
of what you expected from life besides death.

Show me your nothing
that you've left behind
and I'll build from it a forest and a highway,
an airport, baseness, tenderness,
a missing home.

Show me your little poem
and I'll tell you why it wasn't written
any earlier or later than it was.

Oh no, you've got me wrong.
Keep your funny piece of paper
with its scribbles.
All I need for my ends
is your layer of dirt
and the long gone
smell of burning.

VIEW WITH A GRAIN OF SAND

We call it a grain of sand,
but it calls itself neither grain nor sand.
It does just fine without a name,
whether general, particular,
permanent, passing,
incorrect, or apt.

Our glance, our touch mean nothing to it.
It doesn't feel itself seen and touched.
And that it fell on the windowsill
is only our experience, not its.
For it, it is no different from falling on anything else
with no assurance that it has finished falling
or that it is falling still.

The window has a wonderful view of a lake,
but the view doesn't view itself.
It exists in this world
colorless, shapeless,
soundless, odorless, and painless.

The lake's floor exists floorlessly,
and its shore exists shorelessly.
Its water feels itself neither wet nor dry
and its waves to themselves are neither singular nor plural.
They splash deaf to their own noise
on pebbles neither large nor small.

And all this beneath a sky by nature skyless
in which the sun sets without setting at all
and hides without hiding behind an unminding cloud.
The wind ruffles it, its only reason being
that it blows.

A second passes.
A second second.
A third.
But they're three seconds only for us.

Time has passed like a courier with urgent news.
But that's just our simile.
The character is invented, his haste is make-believe,
his news inhuman.

CLOTHES

You take off, we take off, they take off
coats, jackets, blouses, double-breasted suits,
made of wool, cotton, cotton-polyester,
skirts, shirts, underwear, slacks, slips, socks,
putting, hanging, tossing them across
the backs of chairs, the wings of metal screens;
for now, the doctor says, it's not too bad,
you may get dressed, get rested up, get out of town,
take one in case, at bedtime, after lunch,
show up in a couple of months, next spring, next year;
you see, and you thought, and we were afraid that,
and he imagined, and you all believed;
it's time to tie, to fasten with shaking hands
shoelaces, buckles, velcro, zippers, snaps,
belts, buttons, cuff links, collars, neckties, clasps
and to pull out of handbags, pockets, sleeves
a crumpled, dotted, flowered, checkered scarf
whose usefulness has suddenly been prolonged.

ON DEATH, WITHOUT EXAGGERATION

It can't take a joke,
find a star, make a bridge.
It knows nothing about weaving, mining, farming,
building ships, or baking cakes.

In our planning for tomorrow,
it has the final word,
which is always beside the point.

It can't even get the things done
that are part of its trade:
dig a grave,
make a coffin,
clean up after itself.

Preoccupied with killing,
it does the job awkwardly,
without system or skill.
As though each of us were its first kill.

Oh, it has its triumphs,
but look at its countless defeats,
missed blows,
and repeat attempts!

Sometimes it isn't strong enough
to swat a fly from the air.
Many are the caterpillars
that have outcrawled it.

All those bulbs, pods,
tentacles, fins, tracheae,
nuptial plumage, and winter fur
show that it has fallen behind
with its halfhearted work.

Ill will won't help
and even our lending a hand with wars and coups d'état
is so far not enough.

Hearts beat inside eggs.
Babies' skeletons grow.
Seeds, hard at work, sprout their first tiny pair of leaves
and sometimes even tall trees far away.

Whoever claims that it's omnipotent
is himself living proof
that it's not.

There's no life
that couldn't be immortal
if only for a moment.

Death
always arrives by that very moment too late.

In vain it tugs at the knob
of the invisible door.
As far as you've come
can't be undone.

THE GREAT MAN'S HOUSE

The marble tells us in golden syllables:
Here the great man lived, and worked, and died.
Here are the garden paths where he personally scattered the gravel.
Here's the bench—don't touch—he hewed the stone himself.
And here—watch the steps—we enter the house.

He managed to come into the world at what was still a fitting time.
All that was to pass passed in this house.
Not in housing projects,
not in furnished but empty quarters,
among unknown neighbors,
on fifteenth floors
that student field trips rarely reach.

In this room he thought,
in this alcove he slept,
and here he entertained his guests.
Portraits, armchair, desk, pipe, globe,
flute, well-worn carpet, glassed-in porch.
Here he exchanged bows with the tailor and shoemaker
who made his coats and boots to order.

It's not the same as photographs in boxes,
dried-out ballpoint pens in plastic cups,
store-bought clothes in store-bought closets,
a window that looks out on clouds, not passersby.

Was he happy? Sad?
That's not the point.
He still made confessions in letters
without thinking they'd be opened en route.
He still kept a careful, candid diary
knowing it wouldn't be seized in a search.
The thing that most frightened him was a comet's flight.
The world's doom lay then in God's hands alone.

He was lucky enough to die not in a hospital,
not behind some white, anonymous screen.
There was still someone there at his bedside to memorize
his mumbled words.

As if he had been given
a reusable life:
he sent out books to be bound,
he didn't strike the names of the dead from his ledgers.
And the trees that he planted in the garden by his house
still grew for him as *juglans regia*,
and *quercus rubra*, and *ulmus*, and *larix*,
and *fraxinus excelsior*.

IN BROAD DAYLIGHT

                              He would
vacation in a mountain boardinghouse, he would
come down for lunch, from his
table by the window he would
scan the four spruces, branch to branch,
without shaking off the freshly fallen snow.

Goateed, balding,
gray-haired, in glasses,
with coarsened, weary features,
with a wart on his cheek and a furrowed forehead,
as if clay had covered up the angelic marble—he wouldn't
know himself when it all happened.
The price, after all, for not having died already
goes up not in leaps but step by step, and he would
pay that price, too.
About his ear, just grazed by the bullet
when he ducked at the last minute, he would
say: "I was damned lucky."

While waiting to be served his noodle soup, he would
read a paper with the current date,
giant headlines, the tiny print of ads,
or drum his fingers on the white tablecloth, and his hands would
have been used a long time now,
with their chapped skin and swollen veins.

Sometimes someone would
yell from the doorway: "Mr. Baczyński,* phone call for you"—
and there'd be nothing strange about that
being him, about him standing up, straightening his sweater,
and slowly moving toward the door.

---

*Krzysztof Kamil Baczyński, an enormously gifted poet of the "war generation," was killed as a Home Army fighter in the Warsaw Uprising of 1944 at the age of twenty-three. [Translators' note]

At this sight no one would
stop talking, no one would
freeze in mid-gesture, mid-breath
because this commonplace event would
be treated—such a pity—
as a commonplace event.

OUR ANCESTORS' SHORT LIVES

Few of them made it to thirty.
Old age was the privilege of rocks and trees.
Childhood ended as fast as wolf cubs grow.
One had to hurry, to get on with life
before the sun went down,
before the first snow.

Thirteen-year-olds bearing children,
four-year-olds stalking birds' nests in the rushes,
leading the hunt at twenty—
they aren't yet, then they are gone.
Infinity's ends fused quickly.
Witches chewed charms
with all the teeth of youth intact.
A son grew to manhood beneath his father's eye.
Beneath the grandfather's blank sockets the grandson was born.

And anyway they didn't count the years.
They counted nets, pods, sheds, and axes.
Time, so generous toward any petty star in the sky,
offered them a nearly empty hand
and quickly took it back, as if the effort were too much.
One step more, two steps more
along the glittering river
that sprang from darkness and vanished into darkness.

There wasn't a moment to lose,
no deferred questions, no belated revelations,
just those experienced in time.
Wisdom couldn't wait for gray hair.
It had to see clearly before it saw the light
and to hear every voice before it sounded.

Good and evil—
they knew little of them, but knew all:
when evil triumphs, good goes into hiding;
when good is manifest, then evil lies low.
Neither can be conquered
or cast off beyond return.
Hence, if joy, then with a touch of fear;
if despair, then not without some quiet hope.
Life, however long, will always be short.
Too short for anything to be added.

HITLER'S FIRST PHOTOGRAPH

And who's this little fellow in his itty-bitty robe?
That's tiny baby Adolf, the Hitlers' little boy!
Will he grow up to be an L.L.D.?
Or a tenor in Vienna's Opera House?
Whose teensy hand is this, whose little ear and eye and nose?
Whose tummy full of milk, we just don't know:
printer's, doctor's, merchant's, priest's?
Where will those tootsy-wootsies finally wander?
To a garden, to a school, to an office, to a bride?
Maybe to the Bürgermeister's daughter?

Precious little angel, mommy's sunshine, honey bun.
While he was being born, a year ago,
there was no dearth of signs on the earth and in the sky:
spring sun, geraniums in windows,
the organ-grinder's music in the yard,
a lucky fortune wrapped in rosy paper.
Then just before the labor his mother's fateful dream.
A dove seen in a dream means joyful news—
if it is caught, a long-awaited guest will come.
Knock knock, who's there, it's Adolf's heartchen knocking.

A little pacifier, diaper, rattle, bib,
our bouncing boy, thank God and knock on wood, is well,
looks just like his folks, like a kitten in a basket,
like the tots in every other family album.
Sh-h-h, let's not start crying, sugar.
The camera will click from under that black hood.

The Klinger Atelier, Grabenstrasse, Braunau.
And Braunau is a small, but worthy town—
honest businesses, obliging neighbors,

smell of yeast dough, of gray soap.
No one hears howling dogs, or fate's footsteps.
A history teacher loosens his collar
and yawns over homework.

THE CENTURY'S DECLINE

Our twentieth century was going to improve on the others.
It will never prove it now,
now that its years are numbered,
its gait is shaky,
its breath is short.

Too many things have happened
that weren't supposed to happen,
and what was supposed to come about
has not.

Happiness and spring, among other things,
were supposed to be getting closer.

Fear was expected to leave the mountains and the valleys.
Truth was supposed to hit home
before a lie.

A couple of problems weren't going
to come up anymore:
hunger, for example,
and war, and so forth.

There was going to be respect
for helpless people's helplessness,
trust, that kind of stuff.

Anyone who planned to enjoy the world
is now faced
with a hopeless task.

Stupidity isn't funny.
Wisdom isn't gay.
Hope
isn't that young girl anymore,
et cetera, alas.

God was finally going to believe
in a man both good and strong,
but good and strong
are still two different men.

"How should we live?" someone asked me in a letter.
I had meant to ask him
the same question.

Again, and as ever,
as may be seen above,
the most pressing questions
are naïve ones.

CHILDREN OF OUR AGE

We are children of our age,
it's a political age.

All day long, all through the night,
all affairs—yours, ours, theirs—
are political affairs.

Whether you like it or not,
your genes have a political past,
your skin, a political cast,
your eyes, a political slant.

Whatever you say reverberates,
whatever you don't say speaks for itself.
So either way you're talking politics.

Even when you take to the woods,
you're taking political steps
on political grounds.

Apolitical poems are also political,
and above us shines a moon
no longer purely lunar.
To be or not to be, that is the question.
And though it troubles the digestion
it's a question, as always, of politics.

To acquire a political meaning
you don't even have to be human.
Raw material will do,
or protein feed, or crude oil,

or a conference table whose shape
was quarreled over for months:
Should we arbitrate life and death
at a round table or a square one?

Meanwhile, people perished,
animals died,
houses burned,
and the fields ran wild
just as in times immemorial
and less political.

TORTURES

Nothing has changed.
The body is a reservoir of pain;
it has to eat and breathe the air, and sleep;
it has thin skin and the blood is just beneath it;
it has a good supply of teeth and fingernails;
its bones can be broken; its joints can be stretched.
In tortures, all of this is considered.

Nothing has changed.
The body still trembles as it trembled
before Rome was founded and after,
in the twentieth century before and after Christ.
Tortures are just what they were, only the earth has shrunk
and whatever goes on sounds as if it's just a room away.

Nothing has changed.
Except there are more people,
and new offenses have sprung up beside the old ones—
real, make-believe, short-lived, and nonexistent.
But the cry with which the body answers for them
was, is, and will be a cry of innocence
in keeping with the age-old scale and pitch.

Nothing has changed.
Except perhaps the manners, ceremonies, dances.
The gesture of the hands shielding the head
has nonetheless remained the same.
The body writhes, jerks, and tugs,
falls to the ground when shoved, pulls up its knees,
bruises, swells, drools, and bleeds.

Nothing has changed.
Except the run of rivers,
the shapes of forests, shores, deserts, and glaciers.

The little soul roams among those landscapes,
disappears, returns, draws near, moves away,
evasive and a stranger to itself,
now sure, now uncertain of its own existence,
whereas the body is and is and is
and has nowhere to go.

PLOTTING WITH THE DEAD

Under what conditions do you dream of the dead?
Do you often think of them before you fall asleep?
Who appears first?
Is it always the same one?
First name? Surname? Cemetery? Date deceased?

To what do they refer?
Old friendship? Kinship? Fatherland?
Do they say where they come from?
And who's behind them?
And who besides you sees them in his dreams?

Their faces, are they like their photographs?
Have they aged at all with time?
Are they robust? Are they wan?
The murdered ones, have their wounds healed yet?
Do they still remember who killed them?

What do they hold in their hands? Describe these objects.
Are they charred? Moldy? Rusty? Decomposed?
And in their eyes, what? Entreaty? A threat? Be specific.
Do you only chat about the weather?
Or about flowers? Birds? Butterflies?

No awkward questions on their part?
If so, what do you reply?
Instead of safely keeping quiet?
Or evasively changing the dream's subject?
Or waking up just in time?

WRITING A RÉSUMÉ

What needs to be done?
Fill out the application
and enclose the résumé.

Regardless of the length of life,
a résumé is best kept short.

Concise, well-chosen facts are de rigueur.
Landscapes are replaced by addresses,
shaky memories give way to unshakable dates.

Of all your loves, mention only the marriage;
of all your children, only those who were born.

Who knows you matters more than whom you know.
Trips only if taken abroad.
Memberships in what but without why.
Honors, but not how they were earned.

Write as if you'd never talked to yourself
and always kept yourself at arm's length.

Pass over in silence your dogs, cats, birds,
dusty keepsakes, friends, and dreams.

Price, not worth,
and title, not what's inside.
His shoe size, not where he's off to,
that one you pass off as yourself.
In addition, a photograph with one ear showing.
What matters is its shape, not what it hears.
What is there to hear, anyway?
The clatter of paper shredders.

FUNERAL (II)

"so suddenly, who could have seen it coming"
"stress and smoking, I kept telling him"
"not bad, thanks, and you"
"these flowers need to be unwrapped"
"his brother's heart gave out, too, it runs in the family"
"I'd never know you in that beard"
"he was asking for it, always mixed up in something"
"that new guy was going to make a speech, I don't see him"
"Kazek's in Warsaw, Tadek has gone abroad"
"you were smart, you brought the only umbrella"
"so what if he was more talented than they were"
"no, it's a walk-through room, Barbara won't take it"
"of course, he was right, but that's no excuse"
"with body work and paint, just guess how much"
"two egg yolks and a tablespoon of sugar"
"none of his business, what was in it for him"
"only in blue and just small sizes"
"five times and never any answer"
"all right, so I could have, but you could have, too"
"good thing that at least she still had a job"
"don't know, relatives, I guess"
"that priest looks just like Belmondo"
"I've never been in this part of the grounds"
"I dreamed about him last week, I had a feeling"
"his daughter's not bad-looking"
"the way of all flesh"
"give my best to the widow, I've got to run"
"it all sounded so much more solemn in Latin"
"what's gone is gone"
"good-bye"
"I could sure use a drink"

"give me a call"
"which bus goes downtown"
"I'm going this way"
"we're not"

AN OPINION ON THE QUESTION
OF PORNOGRAPHY

There's nothing more debauched than thinking.
This sort of wantonness runs wild like a wind-borne weed
on a plot laid out for daisies.

Nothing's sacred for those who think.
Calling things brazenly by name,
risqué analyses, salacious syntheses,
frenzied, rakish chases after the bare facts,
the filthy fingering of touchy subjects,
discussion in heat—it's music to their ears.

In broad daylight or under cover of night
they form circles, triangles, or pairs.
The partners' age or sex are unimportant.
Their eyes glitter, their cheeks are flushed.
Friend leads friend astray.
Degenerate daughters corrupt their fathers.
A brother pimps for his little sister.

They prefer the fruits
from the forbidden tree of knowledge
to the pink buttocks found in glossy magazines—
all that ultimately simple-hearted smut.
The books they relish have no pictures.
What variety they have lies in certain phrases
marked with a thumbnail or a crayon.

It's shocking, the positions,
the unchecked simplicity with which
one mind contrives to fertilize another!
Such positions the Kama Sutra itself doesn't know.

During these trysts of theirs, the only thing that's steamy is the tea.
People sit on their chairs and move their lips.

Everyone crosses only his own legs
so that one foot is resting on the floor
while the other dangles freely in midair.
Only now and then does somebody get up,
go to the window,
and through a crack in the curtains
take a peep out at the street.

A TALE BEGUN

The world is never ready
for the birth of a child.

Our ships are not yet back from Winnland.
We still have to get over the S. Gothard pass.
We've got to outwit the watchmen on the desert of Thor,
fight our way through the sewers to Warsaw's center,
gain access to King Harald the Butterpat,
and wait until the downfall of Minister Fouché.
Only in Acapulco
can we begin anew.

We've run out of bandages,
matches, hydraulic presses, arguments, and water.
We haven't got the trucks, we haven't got the Minghs' support.
This skinny horse won't be enough to bribe the sheriff.
No news so far about the Tartars' captives.
We'll need a warmer cave for winter
and someone who can speak Harari.

We don't know whom to trust in Nineveh,
what conditions the Prince-Cardinal will decree,
which names Beria has still got inside his files.
They say Karol the Hammer strikes tomorrow at dawn.
In this situation, let's appease Cheops,
report ourselves of our own free will,
change faiths,
pretend to be friends with the Doge,
and say that we've got nothing to do with the Kwabe tribe.

Time to light the fires.
Let's send a cable to grandma in Zabierzów.
Let's untie the knots in the yurt's leather straps.

May delivery be easy,
may our child grow and be well.
Let him be happy from time to time
and leap over abysses.
Let his heart have strength to endure
and his mind be awake and reach far.

But not so far
that it sees into the future.
Spare him
that one gift,
o heavenly powers.

INTO THE ARK

An endless rain is just beginning.
Into the ark, for where else can you go,
you poems for a single voice,
private exultations,
unnecessary talents,
surplus curiosity,
short-range sorrows and fears,
eagerness to see things from all six sides.

Rivers are swelling and bursting their banks.
Into the ark, all you chiaroscuros and half-tones,
you details, ornaments, and whims,
silly exceptions,
forgotten signs,
countless shades of the color gray,
play for play's sake,
and tears of mirth.

As far as the eye can see, there's water and hazy horizon.
Into the ark, plans for the distant future,
joy in difference,
admiration for the better man,
choice not narrowed down to one of two,
outworn scruples,
time to think it over,
and the belief that all this
will still come in handy someday.

For the sake of the children
that we still are,
fairy tales have happy endings.
That's the only finale that will do here, too.
The rain will stop,
the waves will subside,

the clouds will part
in the cleared-up sky,
and they'll be once more
what clouds overhead ought to be:
lofty and rather lighthearted
in their likeness to things
drying in the sun—
isles of bliss,
lambs,
cauliflowers,
diapers.

POSSIBILITIES

I prefer movies.
I prefer cats.
I prefer the oaks along the Warta.
I prefer Dickens to Dostoyevsky.
I prefer myself liking people
to myself loving mankind.
I prefer keeping a needle and thread on hand, just in case.
I prefer the color green.
I prefer not to maintain
that reason is to blame for everything.
I prefer exceptions.
I prefer to leave early.
I prefer talking to doctors about something else.
I prefer the old fine-lined illustrations.
I prefer the absurdity of writing poems
to the absurdity of not writing poems.
I prefer, where love's concerned, nonspecific anniversaries
that can be celebrated every day.
I prefer moralists
who promise me nothing.
I prefer cunning kindness to the overtrustful kind.
I prefer the earth in civvies.
I prefer conquered to conquering countries.
I prefer having some reservations.
I prefer the hell of chaos to the hell of order.
I prefer the Grimms' fairy tales to the newspapers' front pages.
I prefer leaves without flowers to flowers without leaves.
I prefer dogs with uncropped tails.
I prefer light eyes, since mine are dark.
I prefer desk drawers.
I prefer many things that I haven't mentioned here
to many things I've also left unsaid.

I prefer zeros on the loose
to those lined up behind a cipher.
I prefer the time of insects to the time of stars.
I prefer to knock on wood.
I prefer not to ask how much longer and when.
I prefer keeping in mind even the possibility
that existence has its own reason for being.

MIRACLE FAIR

The commonplace miracle:
that so many common miracles take place.

The usual miracle:
invisible dogs barking
in the dead of night.

One of many miracles:
a small and airy cloud
is able to upstage the massive moon.

Several miracles in one:
an alder is reflected in the water
and is reversed from left to right
and grows from crown to root
and never hits bottom
though the water isn't deep.

A run-of-the-mill miracle:
winds mild to moderate
turning gusty in storms.

A miracle in the first place:
cows will be cows.

Next but not least:
just this cherry orchard
from just this cherry pit.

A miracle minus top hat and tails:
fluttering white doves.

A miracle (what else can you call it):
the sun rose today at three fourteen a.m.
and will set tonight at one past eight.

A miracle that's lost on us:
the hand actually has fewer than six fingers
but still it's got more than four.

A miracle, just take a look around:
the inescapable earth.

An extra miracle, extra and ordinary:
the unthinkable
can be thought.

An odd planet, and those on it are odd, too.
They're subject to time, but they won't admit it.
They have their own ways of expressing protest.
They make up little pictures, like for instance this:

At first glance, nothing special.
What you see is water.
And one of its banks.
And a little boat sailing strenuously upstream.
And a bridge over the water, and people on the bridge.
It appears that the people are picking up their pace
because of the rain just beginning to lash down
from a dark cloud.

The thing is, nothing else happens.
The cloud doesn't change its color or its shape.
The rain doesn't increase or subside.
The boat sails on without moving.
The people on the bridge are running now
exactly where they ran before.

It's difficult at this point to keep from commenting.
This picture is by no means innocent.
Time has been stopped here.
Its laws are no longer consulted.
It has been relieved of its influence over the course of events.
It has been ignored and insulted.

On account of a rebel,
one Hiroshige Utagawa
(a being who, by the way,
died long ago and in due course),
time has tripped and fallen down.

It might well be simply a trifling prank,
an antic on the scale of just a couple of galaxies,
let us, however, just in case,
add one final comment for the record:

For generations, it's been considered good form here
to think highly of this picture,
to be entranced and moved.

There are those for whom even this is not enough.
They go so far as to hear the rain's spatter,
to feel the cold drops on their necks and backs,
they look at the bridge and the people on it
as if they saw themselves there,
running the same never-to-be-finished race
through the same endless, ever-to-be-covered distance,
and they have the nerve to believe
that this is really so.

THE END AND THE BEGINNING

1993

SKY

I should have begun with this: the sky.
A window minus sill, frame, and panes.
An aperture, nothing more,
but wide open.

I don't have to wait for a starry night,
I don't have to crane my neck
to get a look at it.
I've got the sky behind my back, at hand, and on my eyelids.
The sky binds me tight
and sweeps me off my feet.

Even the highest mountains
are no closer to the sky
than the deepest valleys.
There's no more of it in one place
than another.
A mole is no less in seventh heaven
than the owl spreading her wings.
The object that falls in an abyss
falls from sky to sky.

Grainy, gritty, liquid,
inflamed, or volatile
patches of sky, specks of sky,
gusts and heaps of sky.
The sky is everywhere,
even in the dark beneath your skin.
I eat the sky, I excrete the sky.
I'm a trap within a trap,
an inhabited inhabitant,
an embrace embraced,
a question answering a question.

Division into sky and earth—
it's not the proper way
to contemplate this wholeness.
It simply lets me go on living
at a more exact address
where I can be reached promptly
if I'm sought.
My identifying features
are rapture and despair.

NO TITLE REQUIRED

It has come to this: I'm sitting under a tree
beside a river
on a sunny morning.
It's an insignificant event
and won't go down in history.
It's not battles and pacts,
where motives are scrutinized,
or noteworthy tyrannicides.

And yet I'm sitting by this river, that's a fact.
And since I'm here
I must have come from somewhere,
and before that
I must have turned up in many other places,
exactly like the conquerors of nations
before setting sail.

Even a passing moment has its fertile past,
its Friday before Saturday,
its May before June.
Its horizons are no less real
than those that a marshal's field glasses might scan.

This tree is a poplar that's been rooted here for years.
The river is the Raba; it didn't spring up yesterday.
The path leading through the bushes
wasn't beaten last week.
The wind had to blow the clouds here
before it could blow them away.

And though nothing much is going on nearby,
the world is no poorer in details for that.
It's just as grounded, just as definite
as when migrating races held it captive.

Conspiracies aren't the only things shrouded in silence.
Retinues of reasons don't trail coronations alone.
Anniversaries of revolutions may roll around,
but so do oval pebbles encircling the bay.

The tapestry of circumstance is intricate and dense.
Ants stitching in the grass.
The grass sewn into the ground.
The pattern of a wave being needled by a twig.

So it happens that I am and look.
Above me a white butterfly is fluttering through the air
on wings that are its alone,
and a shadow skims through my hands
that is none other than itself, no one else's but its own.

When I see such things, I'm no longer sure
that what's important
is more important than what's not.

SOME PEOPLE LIKE POETRY

Some people—
that means not everyone.
Not even most of them, only a few.
Not counting school, where you have to,
and poets themselves,
you might end up with something like two per thousand.

Like—
but then, you can like chicken noodle soup,
or compliments, or the color blue,
your old scarf,
your own way,
petting the dog.

Poetry
but what is poetry anyway?
More than one rickety answer
has tumbled since that question first was raised.
But I just keep on not knowing, and I cling to that
like a redemptive handrail.

THE END AND THE BEGINNING

After every war
someone has to tidy up.
Things won't pick
themselves up, after all.

Someone has to shove
the rubble to the roadsides
so the carts loaded with corpses
can get by.

Someone has to trudge
through sludge and ashes,
through the sofa springs,
the shards of glass,
the bloody rags.

Someone has to lug the post
to prop the wall,
someone has to glaze the window,
set the door in its frame.

No sound bites, no photo opportunities,
and it takes years.
All the cameras have gone
to other wars.

The bridges need to be rebuilt,
the railroad stations, too.
Shirtsleeves will be rolled
to shreds.

Someone, broom in hand,
still remembers how it was.
Someone else listens, nodding
his unshattered head.

But others are bound to be bustling nearby
who'll find all that
a little boring.

From time to time someone still must
dig up a rusted argument
from underneath a bush
and haul it off to the dump.

Those who knew
what this was all about
must make way for those
who know little.
And less than that.
And at last nothing less than nothing.

Someone has to lie there
in the grass that covers up
the causes and effects
with a cornstalk in his teeth,
gawking at clouds.

HATRED

See how efficient it still is,
how it keeps itself in shape—
our century's hatred.
How easily it vaults the tallest obstacles.
How rapidly it pounces, tracks us down.

It's not like other feelings.
At once both older and younger.
It gives birth itself to the reasons
that give it life.
When it sleeps, it's never eternal rest.
And sleeplessness won't sap its strength; it feeds it.

One religion or another—
whatever gets it ready, in position.
One fatherland or another—
whatever helps it get a running start.
Justice also works well at the outset
until hate gets its own momentum going.
Hatred. Hatred.
Its face twisted in a grimace
of erotic ecstasy.

Oh these other feelings,
listless weaklings.
Since when does brotherhood
draw crowds?
Has compassion
ever finished first?
Does doubt ever really rouse the rabble?
Only hatred has just what it takes.

Gifted, diligent, hardworking.
Need we mention all the songs it has composed?

All the pages it has added to our history books?
All the human carpets it has spread
over countless city squares and football fields?

Let's face it:
it knows how to make beauty.
The splendid fire-glow in midnight skies.
Magnificent bursting bombs in rosy dawns.
You can't deny the inspiring pathos of ruins
and a certain bawdy humor to be found
in the sturdy column jutting from their midst.

Hatred is a master of contrast—
between explosions and dead quiet,
red blood and white snow.
Above all, it never tires
of its leitmotif—the impeccable executioner
towering over its soiled victim.

It's always ready for new challenges.
If it has to wait awhile, it will.
They say it's blind. Blind?
It has a sniper's keen sight
and gazes unflinchingly at the future
as only it can.

REALITY DEMANDS

Reality demands
that we also mention this:
Life goes on.
It continues at Cannae and Borodino,
at Kosovo Polje and Guernica.

There's a gas station
on a little square in Jericho,
and wet paint
on park benches in Bila Hora.
Letters fly back and forth
between Pearl Harbor and Hastings,
a moving van passes
beneath the eye of the lion at Chaeronea,
and the blooming orchards near Verdun
cannot escape
the approaching atmospheric front.

There is so much Everything
that Nothing is hidden quite nicely.
Music pours
from the yachts moored at Actium
and couples dance on their sunlit decks.

So much is always going on,
that it must be going on all over.
Where not a stone still stands,
you see the Ice Cream Man
besieged by children.
Where Hiroshima had been
Hiroshima is again,
producing many products
for everyday use.

This terrifying world is not devoid of charms,
of the mornings
that make waking up worthwhile.

The grass is green
on Maciejowice's fields,
and it is studded with dew,
as is normal with grass.

Perhaps all fields are battlefields,
those we remember
and those that are forgotten:
the birch forests and the cedar forests,
the snow and the sand, the iridescent swamps
and the canyons of black defeat,
where now, when the need strikes, you don't cower
under a bush but squat behind it.

What moral flows from this? Probably none.
Only the blood flows, drying quickly,
and, as always, a few rivers, a few clouds.

On tragic mountain passes
the wind rips hats from unwitting heads
and we can't help
laughing at that.

THE REAL WORLD

The real world doesn't take flight
the way dreams do.
No muffled voice, no doorbell
can dispel it,
no shriek, no crash
can cut it short.

Images in dreams
are hazy and ambiguous,
and can generally be explained
in many different ways.
Reality means reality:
that's a tougher nut to crack.

Dreams have keys.
The real world opens on its own
and can't be shut.
Report cards and stars
pour from it,
butterflies and flatiron warmers
shower down,
headless caps
and shards of clouds.
Together they form a rebus
that can't be solved.

Without us dreams couldn't exist.
The one on whom the real world depends
is still unknown,
and the products of his insomnia
are available to anyone
who wakes up.

Dreams aren't crazy—
it's the real world that's insane,
if only in the stubbornness
with which it sticks
to the current of events.

In dreams our recently deceased
are still alive,
in perfect health, no less,
and restored to the full bloom of youth.
The real world lays the corpse
in front of us.
The real world doesn't blink an eye.

Dreams are featherweights,
and memory can shake them off with ease.
The real world doesn't have to fear forgetfulness.
It's a tough customer.
It sits on our shoulders,
weighs on our hearts,
tumbles to our feet.

There's no escaping it,
it tags along each time we flee.
And there's no stop
along our escape route
where reality isn't expecting us.

ELEGIAC CALCULATION

How many of those I knew
(if I really knew them),
men, women
(if the distinction still holds)
have crossed that threshold
(if it is a threshold)
passed over that bridge
(if you can call it a bridge)—

How many, after a shorter or longer life
(if they still see a difference),
good, because it's beginning,
bad, because it's over
(if they don't prefer the reverse),
have found themselves on the far shore
(if they found themselves at all
and if another shore exists)—

I've been given no assurance
as concerns their future fate
(if there is one common fate
and if it is still fate)—

It's all
(if that word's not too confining)
behind them now
(if not before them)—

How many of them leaped from rushing time
and vanished, ever more mournfully, in the distance
(if you put stock in perspective)—

How many
(if the question makes sense,
if one can verify a final sum

without including oneself)
have sunk into that deepest sleep
(if there's nothing deeper)—

See you soon.
See you tomorrow.
See you next time.
They don't want
(if they don't want) to say that anymore.
They've given themselves up to endless
(if not otherwise) silence.
They're only concerned with that
(if only that)
which their absence demands.

CAT IN AN EMPTY APARTMENT

Die—you can't do that to a cat.
Since what can a cat do
in an empty apartment?
Climb the walls?
Rub up against the furniture?
Nothing seems different here,
but nothing is the same.
Nothing has been moved,
but there's more space.
And at nighttime no lamps are lit.

Footsteps on the staircase,
but they're new ones.
The hand that puts fish on the saucer
has changed, too.

Something doesn't start
at its usual time.
Something doesn't happen
as it should.
Someone was always, always here,
then suddenly disappeared
and stubbornly stays disappeared.

Every closet has been examined.
Every shelf has been explored.
Excavations under the carpet turned up nothing.
A commandment was even broken:
papers scattered everywhere.
What remains to be done.
Just sleep and wait.

Just wait till he turns up,
just let him show his face.

Will he ever get a lesson
on what not to do to a cat.
Sidle toward him
as if unwilling
and ever so slow
on visibly offended paws,
and no leaps or squeals at least to start.

PARTING WITH A VIEW

I don't reproach the spring
for starting up again.
I can't blame it
for doing what it must
year after year.

I know that my grief
will not stop the green.
The grass blade may bend
but only in the wind.

It doesn't pain me to see
that clumps of alders above the water
have something to rustle with again.

I take note of the fact
that the shore of a certain lake
is still—as if you were living—
as lovely as before.

I don't resent
the view for its vista
of a sun-dazzled bay.

I am even able to imagine
some non-us
sitting at this minute
on a fallen birch trunk.

I respect their right
to whisper, laugh,
and lapse into happy silence.

I can even allow
that they are bound by love
and that he holds her
with a living arm.

Something freshly birdish
starts rustling in the reeds.
I sincerely want them
to hear it.

I don't require changes
from the surf,
now diligent, now sluggish,
obeying not me.

I expect nothing
from the depths near the woods,
first emerald,
then sapphire,
then black.

There's one thing I won't agree to:
my own return.
The privilege of presence—
I give it up.

I survived you by enough,
and only by enough,
to contemplate from afar.

SÉANCE

Happenstance reveals its tricks.
It produces, by sleight of hand, a glass of brandy
and sits Henry down beside it.
I enter the bistro and stop dead in my tracks.
Henry—he's none other than
Agnes's husband's brother,
and Agnes is related
to Aunt Sophie's brother-in-law.
It turns out
we've got the same great-grandfather.

In happenstance's hands
space furls and unfurls,
spreads and shrinks.
The tablecloth
becomes a handkerchief.
Just guess who I ran into
in Canada, of all places,
after all these years.
I thought he was dead,
and there he was, in Mercedes.
On the plane to Athens.
At a stadium in Tokyo.

Happenstance twirls a kaleidoscope in its hands.
A billion bits of colored glass glitter.
And suddenly Jack's glass
bumps into Jill's.
Just imagine, in this very same hotel.
I turn around and see—
it's really she!
Face to face in an elevator.
In a toy store.
At the corner of Maple and Pine.

Happenstance is shrouded in a cloak.
Things get lost in it and then are found again.
I stumbled on it accidentally.
I bent down and picked it up.
One look and I knew it,
a spoon from that stolen service.
If it hadn't been for that bracelet,
I would never have known Alexandra.
The clock? It turned up in Potterville.

Happenstance looks deep into our eyes.
Our head grows heavy.
Our eyelids drop.
We want to laugh and cry,
it's so incredible.
From fourth-grade homeroom to that ocean liner.
It has to mean something.
To hell and back,
and here we meet halfway home.
We want to shout:
Small world!
You could almost hug it!
And for a moment we are filled with joy,
radiant and deceptive.

LOVE AT FIRST SIGHT

They're both convinced
that a sudden passion joined them.
Such certainty is beautiful,
but uncertainty is more beautiful still.

Since they'd never met before, they're sure
that there'd been nothing between them.
But what's the word from the streets, staircases, hallways—
perhaps they've passed by each other a million times?

I want to ask them
if they don't remember—
a moment face to face
in some revolving door?
perhaps a "sorry" muttered in a crowd?
a curt "wrong number" caught in the receiver?—
but I know the answer.
No, they don't remember.

They'd be amazed to hear
that Chance has beeen toying with them
now for years.

Not quite ready yet
to become their Destiny,
it pushed them close, drove them apart,
it barred their path,
stifling a laugh,
and then leaped aside.

There were signs and signals,
even if they couldn't read them yet.
Perhaps three years ago
or just last Tuesday
a certain leaf fluttered

from one shoulder to another?
Something was dropped and then picked up.
Who knows, maybe the ball that vanished
into childhood's thicket?

There were doorknobs and doorbells
where one touch had covered another
beforehand.
Suitcases checked and standing side by side.
One night, perhaps, the same dream,
grown hazy by morning.

Every beginning
is only a sequel, after all,
and the book of events
is always open halfway through.

MAY 16, 1973

One of those many dates
that no longer ring a bell.

Where I was going that day,
what I was doing—I don't know.

Whom I met, what we talked about,
I can't recall.

If a crime had been committed nearby,
I wouldn't have had an alibi.

The sun flared and died
beyond my horizons.
The earth rotated
unnoted in my notebooks.

I'd rather think
that I'd temporarily died
than that I kept on living
and can't remember a thing.

I wasn't a ghost, after all.
I breathed, I ate,
I walked.
My steps were audible,
my fingers surely left
their prints on doorknobs.

Mirrors caught my reflection.
I wore something or other in such-and-such a color.
Somebody must have seen me.

Maybe I found something that day
that had been lost.
Maybe I lost something that turned up later.

I was filled with feelings and sensations.
Now all that's like
a line of dots in parentheses.

Where was I hiding out,
where did I bury myself?
Not a bad trick
to vanish before my own eyes.

I shake my memory.
Maybe something in its branches
that has been asleep for years
will start up with a flutter.

No.
Clearly I'm asking too much.
Nothing less than one whole second.

MAYBE ALL THIS

Maybe all this
is happening in some lab?
Under one lamp by day
and billions by night?

Maybe we're experimental generations?
Poured from one vial to the next,
shaken in test tubes,
not scrutinized by eyes alone,
each of us separately
plucked up by tweezers in the end?

Or maybe it's more like this:
No interference?
The changes occur on their own
according to plan?
The graph's needle slowly etches
its predictable zigzags?

Maybe thus far we aren't of much interest?
The control monitors aren't usually plugged in?
Only for wars, preferably large ones,
for the odd ascent above our clump of Earth,
for major migrations from point A to B?

Maybe just the opposite:
They've got a taste for trivia up there?
Look! on the big screen a little girl
is sewing a button on her sleeve.
The radar shrieks,
the staff comes at a run.
What a darling little being
with its tiny heart beating inside it!

How sweet, its solemn
threading of the needle!
Someone cries enraptured:
Get the Boss,
tell him he's got to see this for himself!

SLAPSTICK

If there are angels,
I doubt they read
our novels
concerning thwarted hopes.

I'm afraid, alas,
they never touch the poems
that bear our grudges against the world.

The rantings and railings
of our plays
must drive them, I suspect,
to distraction.

Off duty, between angelic—
i.e., inhuman—occupations,
they watch instead
our slapstick
from the age of silent film.

To our dirge wailers,
garment renders,
and teeth gnashers,
they prefer, I suppose,
that poor devil
who grabs the drowning man by his toupee
or, starving, devours his own shoelaces
with gusto.

From the waist up, starch and aspirations;
below, a startled mouse
runs down his trousers.
I'm sure
that's what they call real entertainment.

A crazy chase in circles
ends up pursuing the pursuer.
The light at the end of the tunnel
turns out to be a tiger's eye.
A hundred disasters
mean a hundred comic somersaults
turned over a hundred abysses.

If there are angels,
they must, I hope,
find this convincing,
this merriment dangling from terror,
not even crying Save me Save me
since all of this takes place in silence.

I can even imagine
that they clap their wings
and tears run from their eyes
from laughter, if nothing else.

NOTHING'S A GIFT

Nothing's a gift, it's all on loan.
I'm drowning in debts up to my ears.
I'll have to pay for myself
with my self,
give up my life for my life.

Here's how it's arranged:
The heart can be repossessed,
the liver, too,
and each single finger and toe.

Too late to tear up the terms,
my debts will be repaid,
and I'll be fleeced,
or, more precisely, flayed.

I move about the planet
in a crush of other debtors.
Some are saddled with the burden
of paying off their wings.
Others must, willy-nilly,
account for every leaf.

Every tissue in us lies
on the debit side.
Not a tentacle or tendril
is for keeps.

The inventory, infinitely detailed,
implies we'll be left
not just empty-handed
but handless, too.

I can't remember
where, when, and why

I let someone open
this account in my name.

We call the protest against this
the soul.
And it's the only item
not included on the list.

ONE VERSION OF EVENTS

If we'd been allowed to choose,
we'd probably have gone on forever.

The bodies that were offered didn't fit,
and wore out horribly.

The ways of sating hunger
made us sick.
We were repelled
by blind heredity
and the tyranny of glands.

The world that was meant to embrace us
decayed without end
and the effects of causes raged over it.

Individual fates
were presented for our inspection:
appalled and grieved,
we rejected most of them.

Questions naturally arose, e.g.,
who needs the painful birth
of a dead child
and what's in it for a sailor
who will never reach the shore.

We agreed to death,
but not to every kind.
Love attracted us,
of course, but only love
that keeps its word.

Both fickle standards
and the impermanence of artworks
kept us wary of the Muses' service.

Each of us wished to have a homeland
free of neighbors
and to live his entire life
in the intervals between wars.

No one wished to seize power
or to be subject to it.
No one wanted to fall victim
to his own or others' delusions.
No one volunteered
for crowd scenes and processions,
to say nothing of dying tribes—
although without all these
history couldn't run its charted course
through centuries to come.

Meanwhile, a fair number
of stars lit earlier
had died out and grown cold.
It was high time for a decision.

Voicing numerous reservations,
candidates finally emerged
for a number of roles as healers and explorers,
a few obscure philosophers,
one or two nameless gardeners,
artists and virtuosos—
though even these livings
couldn't all be filled
for lack of other kinds of applications.

It was time to think
the whole thing over.

We'd been offered a trip
from which we'd surely be returning soon,
wouldn't we.

A trip outside eternity—
monotonous, no matter what they say,
and foreign to time's flow.
The chance may never come our way again.

We were besieged by doubts.
Does knowing everything beforehand
really mean knowing everything.

Is a decision made in advance
really any kind of choice.
Wouldn't we be better off
dropping the subject
and making our minds up
once we get there.

We looked at the earth.
Some daredevils were already living there.

A feeble weed
clung to a rock,
trusting blindly
that the wind wouldn't tear it off.

A small animal
dug itself from its burrow
with an energy and hope
that puzzled us.

We struck ourselves as prudent,
petty, and ridiculous.

In any case, our ranks began to dwindle.
The most impatient of us disappeared.
They'd left for the first trial by fire,
this much was clear,
especially by the glare of the real fire

they'd just begun to light
on the steep bank of an actual river.

A few of them
have actually turned back.
But not in our direction.
And with something they seemed to have won in their hands.

WE'RE EXTREMELY FORTUNATE

We're extremely fortunate
not to know precisely
the kind of world we live in.

One would have
to live a long, long time,
unquestionably longer
than the world itself.

Get to know other worlds,
if only for comparison.

Rise above the flesh,
which only really knows
how to obstruct
and make trouble.

For the sake of research,
the big picture
and definitive conclusions,
one would have to transcend time,
in which everything scurries and whirls.

From that perspective,
one might as well bid farewell
to incidents and details.

The counting of weekdays
would inevitably seem to be
a senseless activity;

dropping letters in the mailbox
a whim of foolish youth;

the sign "No Walking on the Grass"
a symptom of lunacy.

NEW POEMS

1993–97

THE THREE ODDEST WORDS

When I pronounce the word Future,
the first syllable already belongs to the past.

When I pronounce the word Silence,
I destroy it.

When I pronounce the word Nothing,
I make something no nonbeing can hold.

SOME PEOPLE

Some people flee some other people.
In some country under a sun
and some clouds.

They abandon something close to all they've got,
sown fields, some chickens, dogs,
mirrors in which fire now preens.

Their shoulders bear pitchers and bundles.
The emptier they get, the heavier they grow.

What happens quietly: someone's dropping from exhaustion.
What happens loudly: someone's bread is ripped away,
someone tries to shake a limp child back to life.

Always another wrong road ahead of them,
always another wrong bridge
across an oddly reddish river.
Around them, some gunshots, now nearer, now farther away,
above them a plane seems to circle.

Some invisibility would come in handy,
some grayish stoniness,
or, better yet, some nonexistence
for a shorter or a longer while.

Something else will happen, only where and what.
Someone will come at them, only when and who,
in how many shapes, with what intentions.
If he has a choice,
maybe he won't be the enemy
and will let them live some sort of life.

A CONTRIBUTION TO STATISTICS

Out of a hundred people

those who always know better
—fifty-two,

doubting every step
—nearly all the rest,

glad to lend a hand
if it doesn't take too long
—as high as forty-nine,

always good
because they can't be otherwise
—four, well maybe five,

able to admire without envy
—eighteen,

suffering illusions
induced by fleeting youth
—sixty, give or take a few,

not to be taken lightly
—forty and four,

living in constant fear
of someone or something
—seventy-seven,

capable of happiness
—twenty-something tops,

harmless singly,
savage in crowds
—half at least,

cruel
when forced by circumstances
—better not to know
even ballpark figures,

wise after the fact
—just a couple more
than wise before it,

taking only things from life
—thirty
(I wish I were wrong),

hunched in pain,
no flashlight in the dark
—eighty-three
sooner or later,

righteous
—thirty-five, which is a lot,

righteous
and understanding
—three,

worthy of compassion
—ninety-nine,

mortal
—a hundred out of a hundred.
Thus far this figure still remains unchanged.

NEGATIVE

Against a grayish sky
a grayer cloud
rimmed black by the sun.

On the left, that is, the right,
a white cherry branch with black blossoms.

Light shadows on your dark face.
You'd just taken a seat at the table
and put your hands, gone gray, upon it.

You look like a ghost
who's trying to summon up the living.

(And since I still number among them,
I should appear to him and tap:
good night, that is, good morning,
farewell, that is, hello.
And not grudge questions to any of his answers
concerning life,
that storm before the calm.)

CLOUDS

I'd have to be really quick
to describe clouds—
a split second's enough
for them to start being something else.

Their trademark:
they don't repeat a single
shape, shade, pose, arrangement.

Unburdened by memory of any kind,
they float easily over the facts.

What on earth could they bear witness to?
They scatter whenever something happens.

Compared to clouds,
life rests on solid ground,
practically permanent, almost eternal.

Next to clouds
even a stone seems like a brother,
someone you can trust,
while they're just distant, flighty cousins.

Let people exist if they want,
and then die, one after another:
clouds simply don't care
what they're up to
down there.

And so their haughty fleet
cruises smoothly over your whole life
and mine, still incomplete.

They aren't obliged to vanish when we're gone.
They don't have to be seen while sailing on.

AMONG THE MULTITUDES

I am who I am.
A coincidence no less unthinkable
than any other.

I could have different
ancestors, after all,
I could have fluttered
from another nest
or crawled bescaled
from under another tree.

Nature's wardrobe
holds a fair supply of costumes:
spider, seagull, field mouse.
Each fits perfectly right off
and is dutifully worn
into shreds.

I didn't get a choice either,
but I can't complain.
I could have been someone
much less separate.
Someone from an anthill, shoal, or buzzing swarm,
an inch of landscape tousled by the wind.

Someone much less fortunate,
bred for my fur
or Christmas dinner,
something swimming under a square of glass.

A tree rooted to the ground
as the fire draws near.

A grass blade trampled by a stampede
of incomprehensible events.

A shady type whose darkness
dazzled some.

What if I'd prompted only fear,
loathing,
or pity?

If I'd been born
in the wrong tribe,
with all roads closed before me?

Fate has been kind
to me thus far.

I might never have been given
the memory of happy moments.

My yen for comparison
might have been taken away.

I might have been myself minus amazement,
that is,
someone completely different.

THE SILENCE OF PLANTS

Our one-sided acquaintance
grows quite nicely.

I know what a leaf, petal, ear, cone, stalk is,
what April and December do to you.

Although my curiosity is not reciprocal,
I specially stoop over some of you,
and crane my neck at others.

I've got a list of names for you:
maple, burdock, hepatica,
mistletoe, heath, juniper, forget-me-not,
but you have none for me.

We're traveling together.
But fellow passengers usually chat,
exchange remarks at least about the weather,
or about the stations rushing past.

We wouldn't lack for topics: we've got a lot in common.
The same star keeps us in its reach.
We cast shadows based on the same laws.
We try to understand things, each in our own way,
and what we don't know brings us closer too.

I'll explain as best I can, just ask me:
what seeing with two eyes is like,
what my heart beats for,
and why my body isn't rooted down.
But how to answer unasked questions,
while being furthermore a being so totally
a nobody to you.

Undergrowth, coppices, meadows, rushes—
everything I tell you is a monologue,
and it's not you who listens.

Talking with you is essential and impossible.
Urgent in this hurried life
and postponed to never.

INDEX OF FIRST LINES